Bunkai Press

Figure 1 Xie Zhen, the Two-headed Snake (Ryotoda Kaichin), from the series One Hundred and Eight Heroes of the Popular Shuihuzhuan (Tsuzoku Suikoden goketsu hyakuhachinin no hitori) 1827-30, Boston Museum of Fine Arts

Suruchin

Flexible Weapon of Okinawan Kobudo

2nd Edition

By

Leo Scott Britt III

Suruchin: Flexible Weapon of Okinawan Kobudo – 2nd Edition

Copyright © 2023 by Leo Scott Britt III

All rights reserved. No part of this book may be reproduced in any form by any electronic or mechanical means including photocopying, recording, or information storage and retrieval without permission in writing from the author.

Cover design by Leo Scott Britt III

Editing by Dr. Olivia Susan Fritts

The adoption and application of material offered in this book is at the reader's discretion and is the reader's sole responsibility. The author and publisher of this book are not responsible for any injury that may occur indirectly or directly from the use or misuse of this book. Use of this book is at the user's own risk and should be overseen by a competent instructor.

ISBN-13: 979-8-474-02653-4

Bunkai Press

Printed in the U.S.A.

Table of Contents

Acknowledgments 7
About the Author 9
Introduction 11
History of the Suruchin (スルチン) 13
    Origins 13
    Ryukyu Kobudo 17
    Matayoshi Kobudo 23
    Meteor Hammer 26
    The Future of the Suruchin 35
Construction of Suruchin 37
    Length 37
    Traditional styles 38
    Modern versions 49
    Practice Suruchin 54
    Constructing a Pocket Suruchin 57
Hojōjutsu (Tying and Binding) 62
    Rope coil 64
    4 Knots 65
    Hayanawa technique – Variant 1 69
    Hayanawa technique – Variant 2 70
Suruchin Techniques 71
    Techniques key 71
    Holds 76
    Swings 85
    Casting/Strikes 97
    Blocks 112
Suruchin Katas 117
    Tan (Short) Suruchin Kata 119

Tan (Short) Suruchin Kata Summary	137
Naga (Long) Suruchin Kata	141
Naga (Long) Suruchin Kata Summary	157
Suruchin no Toseki	161
Suruchin No Toseki Kata Summary	183
Miichiryu Suruchin Kata	187
Miichiryu Summary	211
Suruchin Mini-Kata	215
Kumite	219
Training Methods	231
Resources	235
Index of Figures	237

Acknowledgments

My thanks to those that helped me get this book together – to my wife Mindy, my mother Laurie, my karate students for their constant encouragement and proofreading, and to my aunt Dr. Olivia Susan Fritts for her professional editing services – this would not have been possible without your help. My thanks also go to those that inspired me to create this book through their dedication to the traditional martial arts and the teaching of Bunkai. First and foremost, I want to thank my teacher Keith Cofer for planting a lifelong passion for karate in me, and for serving as a role model and father to me. My thanks also go to those that have served to spread the study of Bunkai to so many – in particular, Pete Mills, Michael Garner, and Ian Abernathy. A special thanks is in order for fellow instructor Jeff Poore (who appears as Uke several places in this book); you have been a great source of help and encouragement, both for this book and for every single class of our martial arts school. This book would not be possible without those who shared with me their time and knowledge of the suruchin weapon during my research for this book, and permission to use various materials (in alphabetical order):

- Andrea Guarelli, 8th dan Matayoshi Kobudo, of the International Matayoshi Kobudō Association
- Angie Spencer, 7th dan Isshinryu, of Spencer's Isshinryu Karate, Virginia
- Bernard Edwards, Chief Master Instructor of the US Karate-Do Hakua Kai Association
- Chris Willson, photographer, of www.travel67.com
- Christian Russo, Jūtaijutsu martial artist and author
- Emile van Heerden, 7th dan Ryukyu Kobudo, Basingstoke England
- Franco Sanguinetti, 8th dan Matayoshi Kobudo, www.bushikan.com
- Hiroshi Akamine, 8th dan Ryukyu Kobudo and 3rd president of Ryukyu Kobudo Hozon Shinkokai
- Juga Paazmaya, photographer, of www.flickr.com/photos/paazio

- Julian Mead, 7th dan Ryukyu Kobudo and Chief instructor and chairman of Ryukyu Kobujutsu Association G.B
- Ken Jack, 2nd dan Ryukyu Kobudo, Indianapolis Dokokai
- Kevin Gurganus, 5th dan Ryukyu Kobudo, Carolina Martial Arts Center
- Kisho Inoue, Ryukyu Kobjutsu Hozon Shinko Kai
- Kuniyoshi Yukio sensei, 8th dan and President of Ryukyu Kobudo Hozon Shiko Kai
- Mario McKenna, 6th dan Ryukyu Kobudo, instructor Vancouver Kowakan school
- Mark D. Bishop, prolific Okinawan karate and kobudo author
- Michael Clayton, president Matayoshi Kobudo Ass. Of Great Britain
- Miguel Da Luz, Okinawa Karate Information Center (http://okic.okinawa)
- Murray Simpson, 8th dan new Zealand under Kiichi Nakamoto Hanshi of Ufuchiku Kobujutsu
- Neil Anderson, of www.antiquechinesesword.com and zhongyimartialarts.org
- Paul Brennan, of brennantranslation.wordpress.com
- Salil Nadkarni, 8th dan Isshinryu and 7th dan Kobudo
- Tomohiro Arashiro, 8th dan Ryuei Ryu
- Victor Donald Smith, master rank Isshinryu, prolific writer
- Yasushi Matayoshi, son of Shinpo Matayoshi, of Matayoshi Kobudo
- Yoshimura Hiroshi, 7th dan Ryukyu Kobudo, chairman of Ryukyu Kobudo Shinkokai

Lastly, a dedication to my grandmother, Lovelle V. Atkisson, who passed in 2020; your influence and love continue to show in my life, and I wish that I could have shown you this completed work. You are very, very missed.

About the Author

At the time of this writing, Scott Britt was a 7th degree black belt in Isshinryu karate, and held rank in Shotokan, Agedo, and Kendo as well. In 2004, he was inducted into the United States Martial Arts Hall of Fame as "Bunkai Instructor of The Year." He has been an avid competitor, with one of his most notable accomplishments being serving on the U.S. team in the 2004 world games in Athens, Greece, where he brought home several medals in various divisions. He was also the 2004 and 2005 U.S. National Martial Arts team Alliance "National Points Champion." In 2012, he was honored to join a team of martial artists going on a mission trip to the Ukraine, where they used their skills and talents to reach others for God.

Scott teaches karate in Oak Ridge, TN, and has a day job as an Instrumentation technician. He, his wife Mindy, and their three sons live in Knoxville, TN. He views karate not as a hobby or as a part-time job, but as a calling and a ministry to help those who are weak become better able to defend themselves, and to introduce Christ and Christian values to those that otherwise may have never had the opportunity to know Him.

Figure 2 1800's Illustration from Water Margin; story written late 14th century.
http://gmzm.org/gudaizihua/shuihurenwu/index.asp?page=15

10

Introduction

This book is the result of countless hours of study and research, during which I sought and compiled information from people across the globe, as well as from out of print and foreign language books. This search crossed multiple styles and lineages. My hope in creating this book is that other martial artists learning the suruchin will have a succinct, single source for all the knowledge and katas I have pieced together from dozens of sources.

The suruchin is a fascinating weapon. It is a lesser-known weapon in the category of flexible weapons. Unlike other traditional Kobudo weapons it can be hidden or concealed; it can also be improvised from such things as power cords and tow straps and is highly portable. These qualities make it an excellent candidate for study in modern times.

Figure 3 Tiara Shinken

I also hope to further the art of suruchin in a practical sense, adding in what I have developed through the careful study of the three main styles that utilize the suruchin. These additions to the global suruchin knowledge base (Miichiryu suruchin kata, modern construction techniques, etc.) are clearly labeled as such in this book and should give the reader additional grist for the mill.

I hope the reader enjoys this content and finds it easily understandable and relevant. I have striven to be both accurate and comprehensive; however, should the reader discover any inaccuracies or know of additional information not provided in this book, please contact me at isshin-ryu@hotmail.com and I will gladly incorporate these comments into any future editions.

History of the Suruchin (スルチン)

Origins

As with most topics related to martial arts, there is only so far back the written record goes before events are lost to history. It is believed that the suruchin (also spelled Surujin, or less commonly Surichin) in some form started in the ancient past as a hunting weapon, possibly thrown in a similar manner to the South American Bolas used by the gauchos (Argentinian cowboys). While maintaining hold of one end, it basically becomes a way of hunting small animals by casting a weight which can then be quickly recovered to be recast. From there, it was used through the centuries by various armies under different names, in part because of its effectiveness for and against mounted soldiers.

As far as the Okinawan history of the weapon, Mikio Nishiuchi of Matayoshi Kobudo presents several possible origins for the suruchin and its name [13]:

a) Surukaa = bark/hemp rope, chin = weights used to hold paper down while brush writing
b) Surukaa = bark/hemp = rope, chin = to make peaceful
c) Weighted ropes used to hold down shingles on a roof
d) Weighted rope added to fishing net for fishing in deep waters (see photo pg. 16)

Meanwhile, Mark Bishop [2] suggests that the origin was often claimed to be the balance/weights used by Okinawan shopkeepers and merchants, though he points out that there is not a perfect carryover in size/weight to the suruchin. However, this is also the version heard by Kuniyoshi Yukio of Ryukyu Kobudo.

Lastly, the Meteor hammer section of this book describes the possibility that the Okinawan practitioners of the suruchin may have been inspired by the Shaolin weapons of China.

Figure 4 Boys with Suruchin, from nanto zatsuwa (1880)

There are two primary martial art styles that use the suruchin: Ryukyu Kobudo (through Taira Shinken) and Matayoshi Kobudo (through Shinpo Matayoshi). There is a third style to be counted, Shaolin kung Fu, whose double-sided meteor hammer is mostly different in name only. These three styles have surprisingly little overlap in techniques and kata, each offering a different perspective on the weapon.

In addition to these main styles for suruchin, another deserves mention. Ryūei-ryū was originally the family style of the Nakaima family of Naha. It was founded by Norisato Nakaima (1819-1879) and passed down to his son Nakaima Kenchu (1856-1953). While there are references to the suruchin being included in the weapons list, the official stance is that the suruchin is not practiced in the style in modern times. No known suruchin katas exist in Ryūei-ryū.

Lastly, some sources mention other styles such as Matsumura Orthadox Shorin-ryu, Koryu Kobudo, and Ufuchiku kobudo practicing suruchin [2,3,12]. However, research has been unable to find examples of the weapon in use in modern times in these styles.

Figure 5 Ufuchiku, who reportedly practiced suruchin [12]

Figure 6 Taira Shinken, Motokatsu Inoue, Higa Seiko, and Matayoshi Shinpo (1960)

Figure 7 Fishing net and weights detail from Karwar, courtesy of Salil Nadkarni

Ryukyu Kobudo

Sometimes called the father of Okinawan Kobudo, Taira Shinken carefully studied and cataloged the traditional weapon katas of the Ryukyu islands, while also at times creating katas to document techniques when no traditional katas were in existence. He is credited with preserving 42 weapons katas, covering Bo, Sai, Tonfa, Nunchaku, Kama, Tekko, Tinbe-rochin, Eku, and Suruchin. Taira had the given name Shinken Maezato (he took his mother's name Taira later), so in accordance with the tradition of naming katas after their originator, some katas connected with Taira are called Maezato no Tekko or the like.

Much of Taira Shinken's kobudo was learned under Moden Yabiku, founder of the Ryukyu Kobujutsu Kenkyu Kai (Ryukyu Kobujutsu Research Association). However, it is Taira Shinken's grandfather Kanegawa Gimu (or Gibu) who is credited with introducing him to the suruchin weapon. Not much is known about Kanegawa Gimu, other than that he was a high-ranking official in the Ryuku kingdom government. After the Riuki's affiliation with Japan, he lost his job and had to survive from farming and fishing. He was a master of nichou kama (double kama), tekko, suruchin, and tinbe [6]. Contradicting this is an account [9] that states Taira was taught by Master Yafuso (no full name known), a disciple of Taira's grandfather. However, this being said, it is impossible to fully isolate Taira Shinken's suruchin influences as he spent his lifetime learning the techniques and katas of countless people across Okinawa.

In 1940, shortly before the death of Yabiku Sensei in 1941, Taira established the Ryukyu Kobudo Hozon Shinko-Kai, the association for the preservation and promotion of Ryukyu Kobudo based in Naha, built on the organization of Yabiku Sensei's Ryukyu Kobujutsu Kenkyu Kai [9]. While Taira hoped to write several books, the only book produced before his death in 1970 was Ryukyu Kobudo Taikan in 1964 (translated into English [14,18]).

This brief book unfortunately only has an introductory paragraph for the suruchin.

Upon Taira's passing, Eisuke Akamine took over the style in Okinawa, followed by Akamine Hiroshi. The current head of the Ryukyu Kobudo Hozon Shinko Kai is Yukio Kuniyoshi. Meanwhile, Motokatsu Inoue was the head in Japan after Taira's death. Motokatsu published several books to document the katas of Ryukyu Kobudo [10,11]. The first volume of his Ryukyu Kobujutsu trilogy has the Long suruchin kata documented, while the third (as well as his English book Ryukyu Kobujutsu [Chi no maki]) has the short suruchin kata. His son Kisho Inoue is the current head of the Ryukyu Kobujutsu Hozon Shinko Kai and Yuishinkai organization in Tokyo. The following lineage is restricted to suruchin history and does not include all influences on the style.

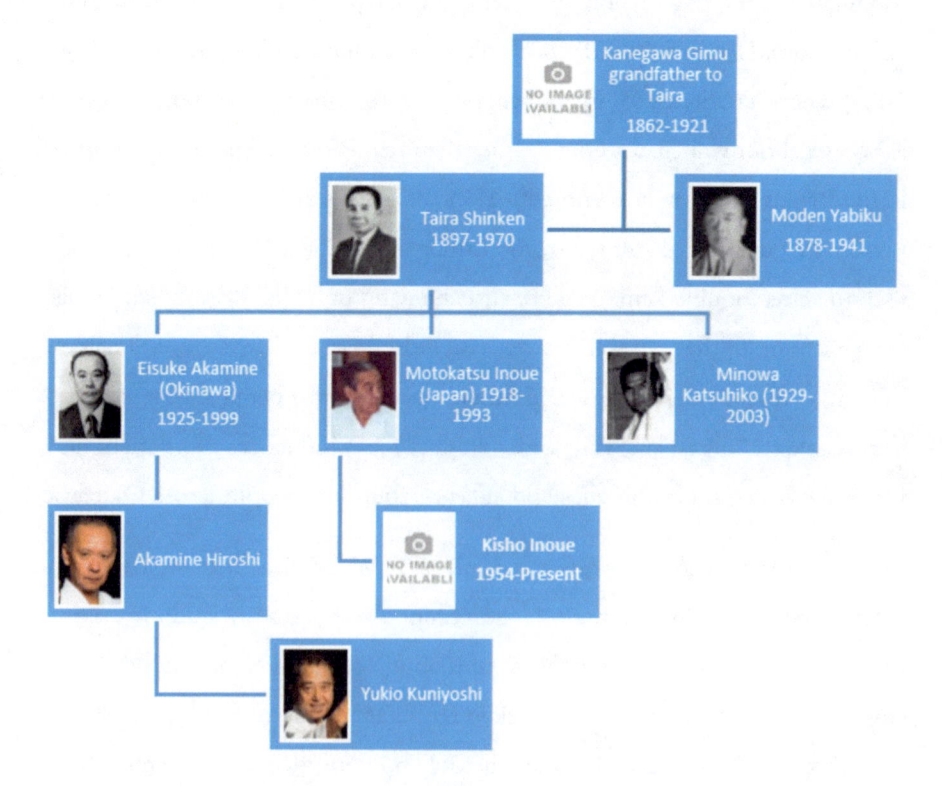

Figure 8 Ryukyu Kobudo lineage

There is some controversy around the exact origin of the two suruchin katas, Naga (long) suruchin and Tan (short) suruchin. Some people interviewed have stated that Taira only practiced Waza (techniques) and did not do any kata. Written sources [21] have Naga suruchin created by Taira Shinken himself, while the Tan suruchin kata was created by Minowa Katsuhiko (called Maezato no suruchin and Minowa no suruchin). However, in interviews for research for this book, 7th dan Yoshimura Hiroshi of Ryukyu Kobudo Shinko Kai (student of Minowa) states that both katas are the creation of Motokatsu Inoue, and that Maezato Suruchin is a separate kata (no example found of a different kata). Meanwhile, Kisho Inoue, the current head of Ryukyu Kobujutsu Hozon Shinko Kai, states that both kata are handed down from Taira Shinken's grandfather, Kanegawa Gimu. It is the author's theory that the long kata was created by Taira, and the short by one of his students, either Motokatsu (since it is highlighted in his books over the long kata and is the only kata with video of himself performing it) or Katsuhiko. This was likely done with the blessing of Taira himself (and possibly his guidance), and then incorporated into the style. However, with no written record from Taira himself, this is only a theory.

Figure 9 Taira Shinken

Figure 10 Eisuke Akamine

Figure 11 Motokatsu Inoue

Figure 12 Akamine Hiroshi

Figure 13 Yukio Kuniyoshi

Permission not received to include photo of master Inoue in lineage.

Figure 14 Kisho Inoue

Figure 15 Moden Yabiku

Figure 16 Minowa Katsuhiko

21

Matayoshi Kobudo

The other main style to practice suruchin is Matayoshi Kobudo. The founder, Shinko Matayoshi, was ancestor to the well known Okinawan lord Shinjo Gima, and learned Kobudo weapons from his father Matayoshi Shinchin, as well as Agena Chokubo and Ire Okina. However, it was on a trip to China that he became acquainted with the suruchin. In 1905 at the age of 17, he left Okinawa on his way to China. He ended up stopping in the Manchuria area for 2-3 years and living with a band of mounted nomads/bandits. After moving on, he ended up in Fuchow city, in Fujian province, where he trained under Kingai Roshi, who taught him the Kingai-ryu style [7,8].

It is here that sources start to disagree regarding the suruchin; some state that he learned the Bola (suruchin-like weapon) from the nomads, along with the lasso and Shuriken. Other sources say that he learned suruchin along with tinbei, and nunti from Kingai Roshi [5]. Whichever is accurate, there was no kata for the suruchin at this point, but a collection of techniques.

Shinko's son, Shinpo Matayoshi, carried on the tradition of Kobudo. Shinpo taught the basics and each student arranged it. Seiko Itakazo is the person credited with creating the Suruchin kata of Matayoshi Kobudo, "Suruchin no Toseki" (throwing the stone), though some suggest it may have been Kenichi Yamashiro. It is also of interest that some students of the 1960s have known Shinpo Matayoshi to use a single-ended suruchin (like the single-ended meteor hammer of today). A good example of the suruchin kata can be seen in the film "Matayoshi Shinpo's Traditional Okinawan Kobudo" [19].

The current descendant of Matayoshi Kobudo is Yasushi Matayoshi. Several direct students of Shinpo Matayoshi have branched out with their own organizations; of note are Kenishi Yamashiro and Andrea Guarelli, (next page) who have modified versions of the suruchin kata. The following lineage is restricted to suruchin history and does not include all influences on the style.

Figure 17 Kenichi Yamashiro

Figure 18 Andrea Guarelli

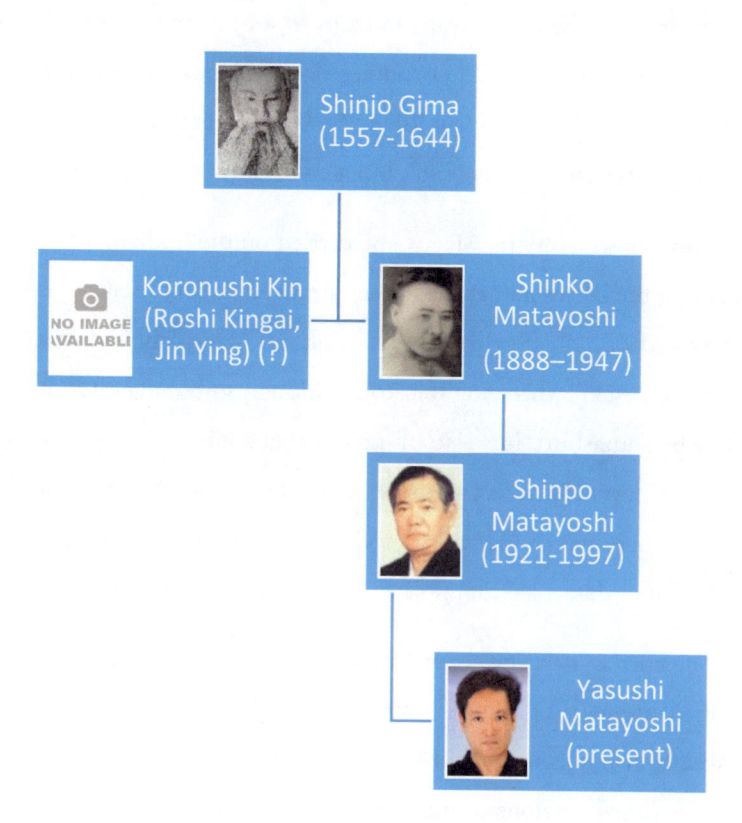

Figure 19 Matayoshi Kobudo lineage

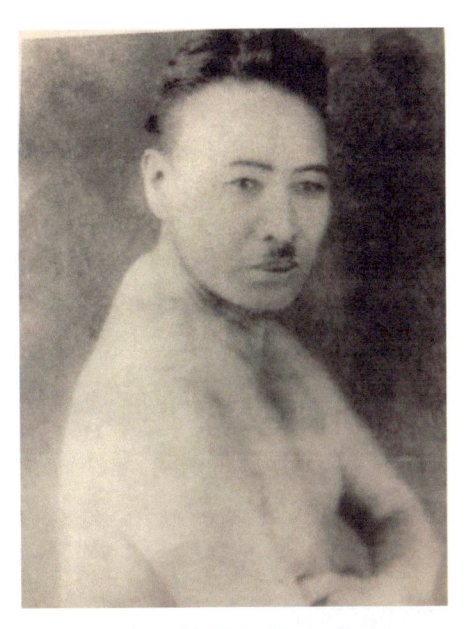

Figure 20 Shinko Matayoshi

Figure 21 Shinpo Matayoshi

Figure 22 Shinjo Gima Portrait

Figure 23 Yasushi Matayoshi

25

Meteor Hammer

Found in Shaolin Kung Fu and Wushu, the meteor hammer (also called dai chui, flying hammer, or dragon's fist) is close kin to the suruchin.

There are two kinds of meteor hammer: the single-ended version, usually about 5 meters in length, and the double-ended version which is about two meters in length (which most closely resembles the traditional suruchin). While the single-ended version is the more popular one today, the double meteor hammer has one of the oldest references of any suruchin-like weapon.

Figure 24 Meteor Hammer - By Samuraiantiqueworld - Own work, CC BY-SA 3.0, https://commons.wikimedia.org/w/index.php?curid=12682113

The following page is from volume 104 of the Wubei Zhi ("Records of Military Training"), also called the Bubishi, written in 1621 [20]; it reads:

> Flying hammers, also called "meteor hammers," are used in pairs. The one held in the front hand is the "direct hammer" and the other held lifted in the rear hand is the "emergency hammer" (translation courtesy of Paul Brennan, brennantranslation.wordpress.com).

飛鎚即流星鎚也　一前者爲之正鎚後面手中提者爲之救命鎚

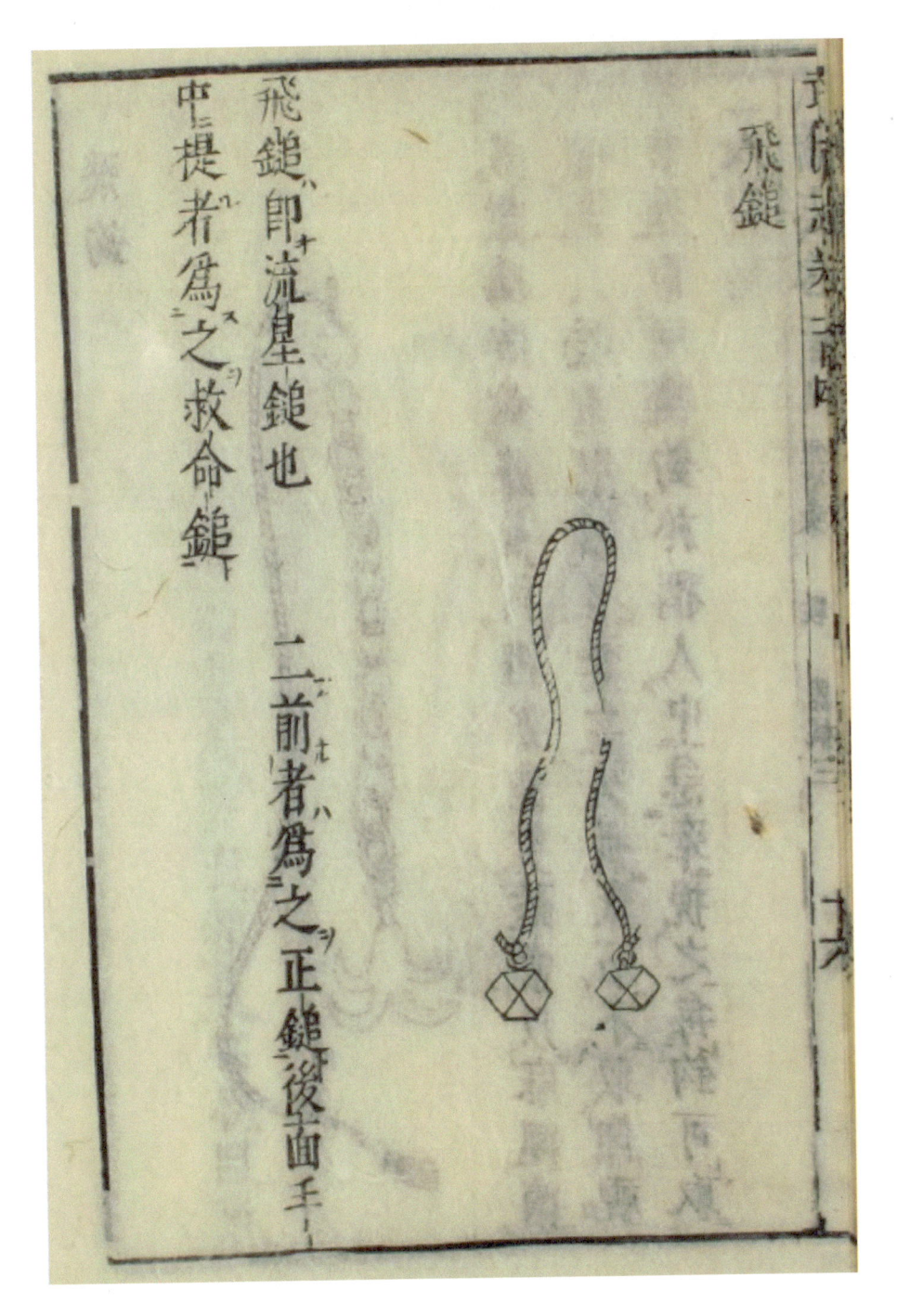

飛鎚

Figure 25 Wubei Zhi 1621 - meteor hammers

The weights for antique meteor hammers have several designs: gourd, garlic head, and tetradechahedron shapes, made of copper, brass, brass-studded wood, and iron. Weights average around 1lb, up to 2lb (much heavier than modern remakes). See below for a representative sample of end weights. The Shaolin meteor hammer, like several other schools of soft weapons, do not have a strict kata or form (like some schools of Manriki fundo), but rather a collection of techniques.

Figure 26 Example of various Chinese meteor hammer end weights, later Qing era. Courtesy of the Neil Anderson Collection, of antiquechinesesword.com

Figure 27 Later Qing era garlic head mace, brass 14.1oz. Courtesy of the Neil Anderson Collection, of antiquechinesesword.com

28

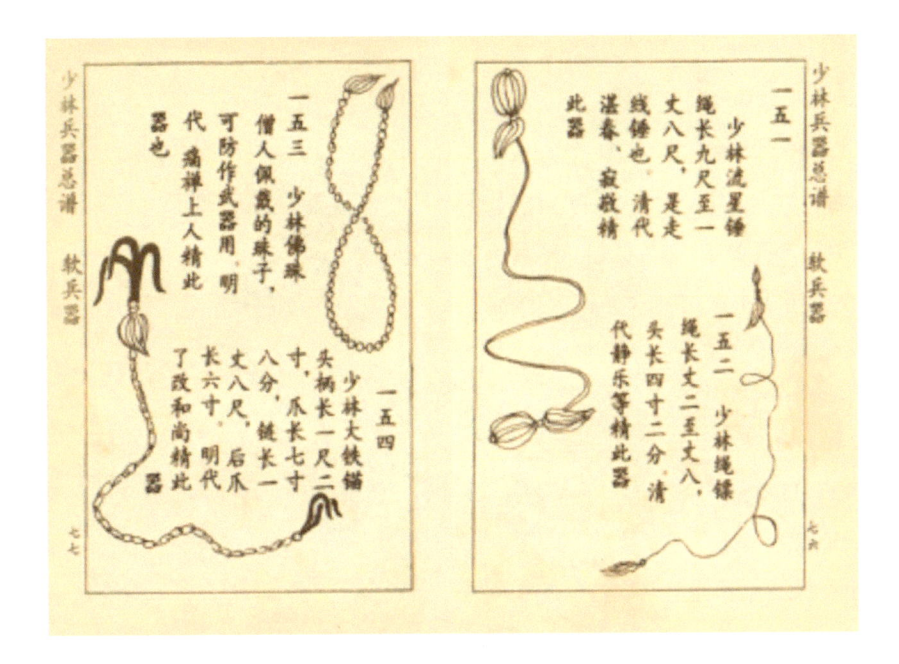

Figure 28 Engraving describing Shaolin 8-9ft meteor hammer of Qing dynasty.

The double-ended meteor hammer has also seen use for street performance, both in modern times and in times past, as can be seen by this early 19th century painting:

Figure 29 Meteor hammer painting. Courtesy of the Neil Anderson Collection, of antiquechinesesword.com

29

The meteor hammer is mentioned in the *Water Margin* story (late 14th century) as well as *Romance of the Three Kingdoms* (circa 1322), two of four novels considered to be the four great classical novels of Chinese literature. However, the origin of the meteor hammer likely stretches back significantly further, with author Dr. Yang [22] suggesting it may have been developed as early as the Tang dynasty (618-907 A.D.).

Figure 30 Xie Zhen, the Two-headed Snake (Ryotoda Kaichin), from the series One Hundred and Eight Heroes of the Popular Shuihuzhuan (Tsuzoku Suikoden goketsu hyakuhachinin no hitori) 1827-30, Boston Museum of Fine Arts

Of note in these stories are the descriptions of its use, including a mounted soldier using a meteor hammer to strike backwards at a pursuing mounted enemy.

The use of the meteor hammer by mounted soldiers has a modern equivelent; the Bola is a nearly identical weapon used by many groups in Patagonia (South America), in particular the Gauchos (cowboys) of Argentina. While several styles of Bola were used, ones identical to suruchin and meteor hammer were used from horseback to hunt rheas as shown in the following illustration.

30

Figure 31 Emeric Essex Vidal (1791-1861), Public domain, via Wikimedia Commons

As mentioned, the single-sided meteor hammer is by far the most common meteor hammer used today. The single-ended version can be up to 20 feet in length, with one end of the rope including a loop for the practitioner to place around the wrist. Of interest is Yugen Budo Shinkokai, a style in France founded in 1986 that has applied suruchin techniques to the single-ended meteor hammer (http://oudekrijgskunsten.nl/), complete with the katas O-kusari kata and Ishiguro no suruchin.

Lastly, while there is no definitive proof or record, it is the author's strong belief that the meteor hammer was the precursor and inspiration for the Okinawan suruchin. While it is possible that they were developed independently of each other, the fact that Okinawa was a major shipping hub and a melting pot due to the constant stream of travelers, combined with Shinko Matayoshi's travels through China, lends credence to the idea that the Okinawans saw the meteor hammer, and adopted/adapted it to their Kobudo weapons list. This would be no more than what happened constantly with the open hand katas of martial arts; for instance, several Okinawan katas have roots in white crane kung fu, though they have been modified to the point of becoming their own entity. A perfect example of this development in action is the Rante; the Chinese-inspired weapon of Delima Silat, an Indonesian martial art [4]. A light chain with 2oz weights added to ends, this weapon is like the suruchin in that it is basically a double ended meteor hammer with a local name applied.

Figure 32 Illustration from the Water Margin story, Shui hu ren wu quan tu by Du Jin, 1467-1487

Figure 33 Illustration from History of the Three Kingdoms, 1368-1644, World Digital Library

Figure 34 Rante of Indonesia [4], Copyright © 1972 by Charles E Tuttle Publishing Co., Inc.

The Future of the Suruchin

Due to several likely factors, such as focusing on the more common weapons (e.g., Bo) and lack of dojo space, the suruchin in most schools is not learned until black belt, and in many schools (Ryukyu Kobudo and Matayoshi Kobudo both included) it is reserved for after Go-Dan (5th degree black belt), or as an optional kata. One of the given reasons for this is that suruchin is a more difficult weapon to master; unfortunately, this policy has resulted in the suruchin becoming in danger of going extinct. In researching for this book for example, many of the "ambassador instructors" for a style to other countries did not know their style's suruchin kata. Even the head of one of the branches of Ryukyu Kobudo could not provide an example of the long suruchin kata (Naga Suruchin) being run, effectively making it a dead kata in that branch. While the suruchin is a more difficult weapon to master than say, the Bo, this weapon can still be easily learned by practitioners of all ages and ranks as has been proven in the author's dojo.

It is the author's opinion that the suruchin needs to move to an earlier point in the curriculum of Kobudo schools to prevent it from eventually going extinct altogether as masters pass away. Some of these Kobudo styles have 11 kata just for Bo; surely the suruchin, this fascinating and unique weapon, can be moved up the list for posterity's sake. With this in mind be sure to read the introduction to the Mini kata section provided later in this book.

Construction of Suruchin

Length

There are a large variety of lengths used traditionally. Ryukyu Kobudo with the handle-style suruchin will usually use 5 shaku (150-152cm) for a short suruchin (from end of weight to start of handle, excluding handle) and eight shaku (230-240cm) for a long suruchin (again, excluding the handle). Matayoshi Kobudo has been known to use three, five, six, and eight shaku length suruchins (90.9cm, 151cm, 181cm, and 240cm).

However, especially due to the differing sizes of karate students, the author prefers the method of measuring set out by Mikio Nishiuchi of Matayoshi Kobudo. This involves measuring the weapon specific to the user, at 1.5x arm span. See below for example. This is a similar length and method of measurement to the Shaolin meteor hammer.

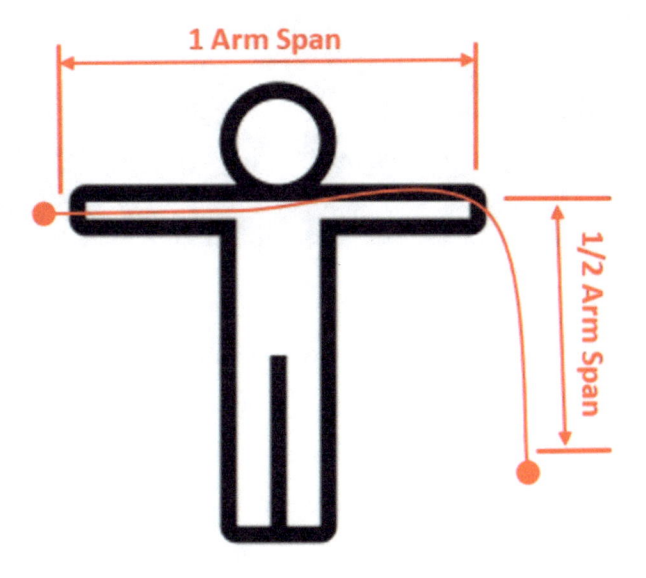

Figure 35 Suruchin length

Traditional styles

Rope Suruchin

Figure 36 Rope and Stone Suruchin, author's collection

Rope suruchins are the type more commonly used in Matayoshi Kobudo. They are made from hemp rope (which has a much higher breaking strength than a jute rope of the same diameter), with two river rocks serving as the weights. The rocks should be flat, preferably teardrop shaped, and approximately 6-10oz and 2-2.5" x 2.5-3.5". The rocks require a diamond drill bit to make the holes. The rope is then threaded through the rocks and spliced back into itself and whipped at the end. Note that splicing retains the full strength of the rope, while any type of knot will create a weak spot in the rope.

Additional Examples of Rope Suruchin

Figure 37 Metal weights, courtesy of Todd Ward

Figure 38 Additional example of rope suruchin

Figure 39 Rope suruchin with Matayoshi style handle, courtesy of Todd Ward

39

Hag Stones

While the ability to carve and shape stone has been around for thousands of years, it is worth noting the existence of stones with naturally occurring holes in them. These holes can be a result of the boring of a bivalve mollusk called a 'piddock,' two stones grinding together, or imperfections in the stone that wear away in the water at a different rate to the main material. There are various myths surrounding these stones worldwide, from British tales of looking through the hole to see the world of the fairies, to Russian tales of the stones being abodes of Kurinyi Bog spirits (guardians of chickens). Even the historian Pliny tells of the stones being prized by Roman druids.

In Asia, these stones are sought out as Scholar's stones (or Viewing stones), known as Gongshi in China and Suiseki in Japan. These are naturally occurring rocks set on a small wooden base for ornamental purposes.

Figure 40 Dr.mgf.winkelmann, Copyrighted free use, via Wikimedia Commons

Figure 41 Hag stone, authors collection - from USA East coast

Chain Suruchin

The chain suruchin, usually with a handle on one end, is typically used by the Ryukyu Kobudo style. It can be manufactured several different ways, with the original ones being hand forged. As can be seen in next image, they were also occasionally made with backward spikes on the end, allowing the weight to grip and hold when wrapping around a target. A consideration if making a chain suruchin: the chain must be significantly lighter than the weight at the end. Otherwise, the suruchin will handle like a single long heavy chain and will not behave properly on casting techniques.

Figure 42 Traditional chain suruchins of karatekobudopalau.com

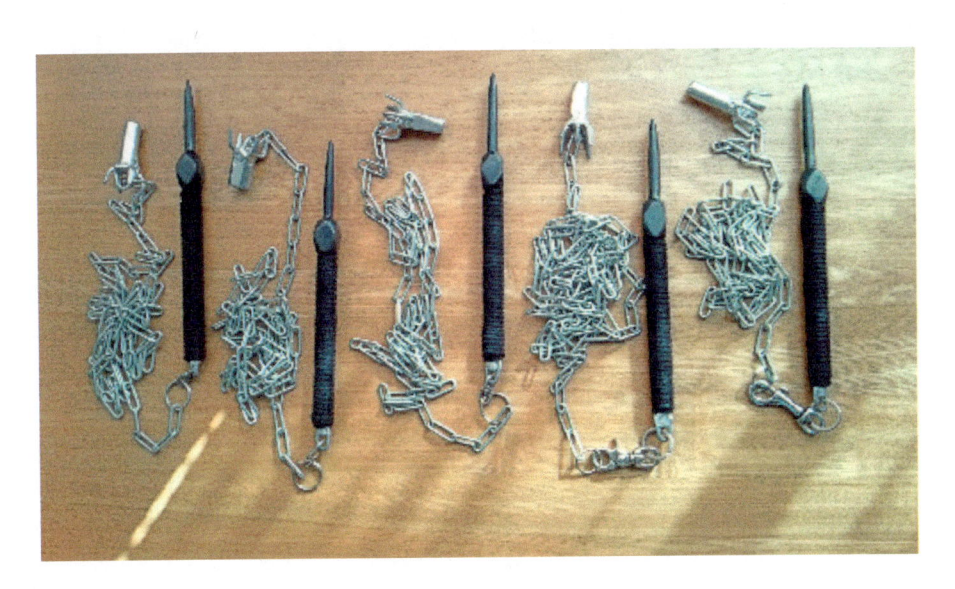

Figure 43 Suruchin with barbs, courtesy of http://bushukan.wp.xdomain.jp/

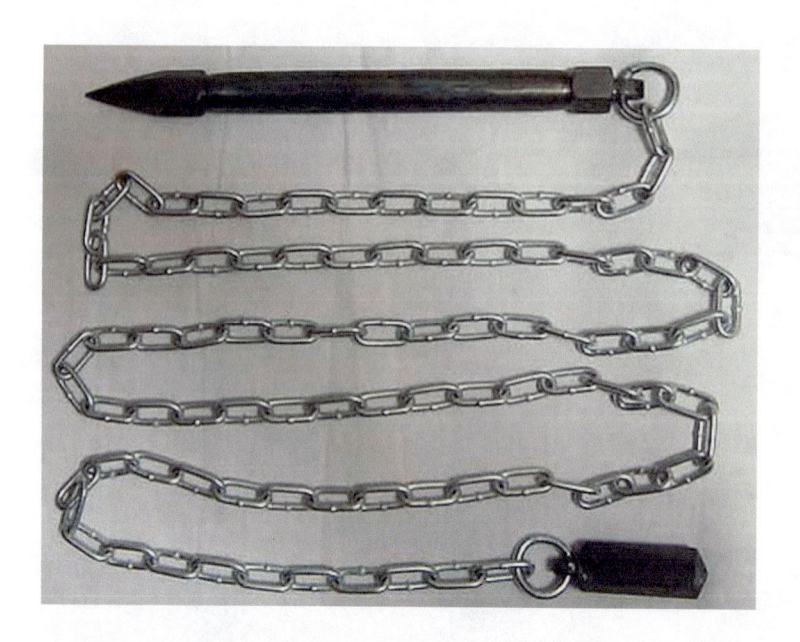

Figure 44 suruchin from jin-1.juttemaster.gozaru.jp

Figure 45 Taira lineage suruchins, of ryukyukobujutsuhozonshinkokai.org

Figure 46 Chain Suruchin Photo: paazio / flickr

    The photo above (courtesy of Juga Paazmaya of Flickr, www.flickr.com/photos/paazio) shows an example of a handle that tapers to a point. While this adds a dimension to using the handle in the manner of a Yawara or Kubaton, it also opens up the possibility of reversing the grip on the suruchin and utilizing Rope Dart techniques.

Figure 47 Suruchin made from Manriki

The photo above shows a suruchin made from commercially available Manriki weapons cut apart (one handle version, one ball version) with 1/8 inch chain added with steel quick links.

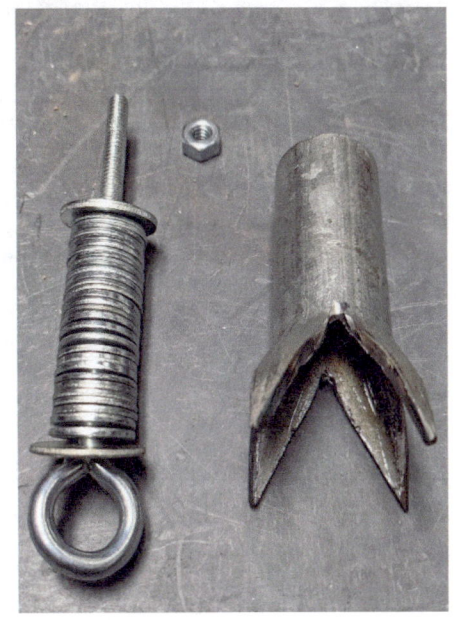

Figure 48 Barbed suruchin, with details of construction

Barbed suruchin using metal pipe, eyelet bolt, and washers. Excess bolt removed with grinder. Nut epoxied in place.

47

Figure 49   Top Left: Meteor hammer style handle.   Top Right: Barbed end.   Bottom: Chain suruchin. Courtesy of Todd Ward

48

Modern versions

Figure 50 Modern monkey fist suruchin

The photo above shows a rope suruchin constructed using 1.5" steel ball bearings wrapped in a monkey fist knot (ABoK #2202). The rope is 5.6mm Atwood "Battle Cord" rope, with a tensile strength of 2,650lbs. The remaining end of rope from each knot is tied back into the standing end using a Celtic button knot (ABoK #545). A drop of epoxy on the Celtic button knots helps ensure it never comes unraveled. Below is a youth sized suruchin, using traditional hemp rope and 3/4" steel ball bearings in a monkey fist:

Figure 51 Youth Hemp suruchin

Figure 52 Iron ball and Dyneema® Suruchin

The suruchin above is constructed using 3/16" Dyneema® hollow core rope (7000lb). The ends are 1.5" cast iron balls prepared as follows:

1. Drill ¼" hole through iron ball (drill press and vice ideal)
2. Widen hole at one end to 9/16" wide by 1/2" deep
3. Insert eyebolt and fasten with nylon locking nut; a flat head screwdriver wedged in the hole helps to tighten the nut until it is below the surface of the hole in the iron ball
4. Cut off excess bolt with grinder/cutting wheel
5. Fill in the hole with "J-B Weld 8265S Original Cold-Weld Steel Reinforced Epoxy"
6. Thread rope loop (see below) through eye bolt and pass around ball

This Suruchin is the author's personal favorite for everyday practice; the Suruchin is industrial strength and will not come apart, and the Dyneema® rope is smooth to the touch. This Suruchin requires a specific type of splice to make the loops: the Brummel locking splice with one end secured. Since this may not be known to all people and is not in the Ashley Book of Knots, the following pages details how to make this splice.

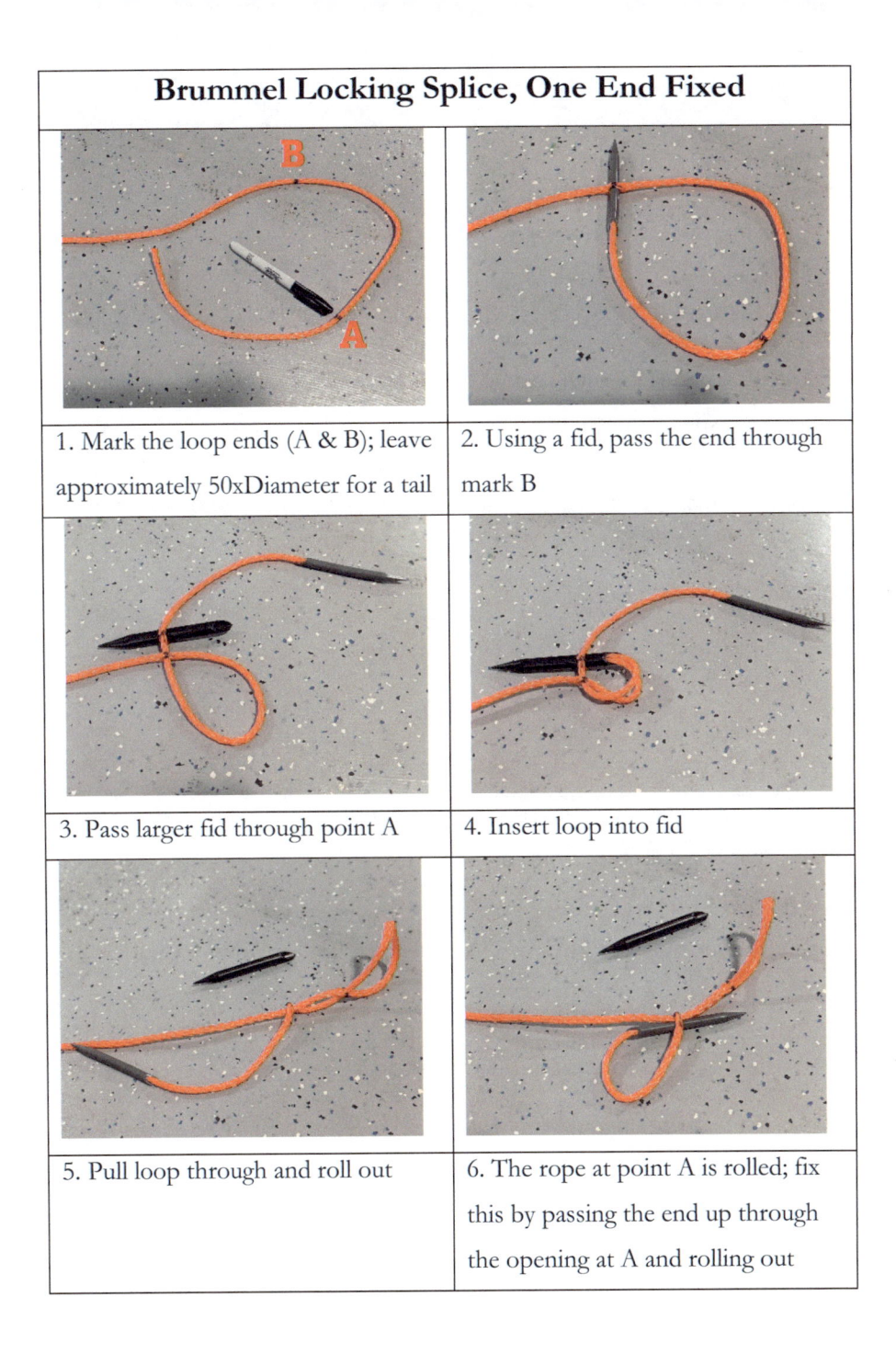

Brummel Locking Splice, One End Fixed

1. Mark the loop ends (A & B); leave approximately 50xDiameter for a tail	2. Using a fid, pass the end through mark B
3. Pass larger fid through point A	4. Insert loop into fid
5. Pull loop through and roll out	6. The rope at point A is rolled; fix this by passing the end up through the opening at A and rolling out

 7. The rope passes through itself at two points; spread open loop to bring these together and lock knot	 8. To finish off, take the end fid and enter the hollow core of the rope about 1/4" above the locked knot
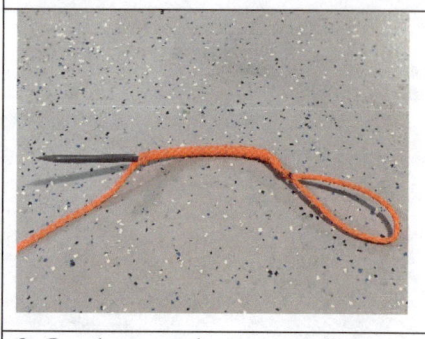 9. Continue up the rope until you are longer than the tail, then exit to the side. Remove fid and allow tail to be left fully inside hollow core	 10. Finished splice. Note: some prefer to pick apart the end of the tail and use a razor to taper the end at step 9 for a smother feeling transition

Figure 53 Kashaka style suruchin

      Designed for tournament, the suruchin above is made of hollow steel spheres with a couple of ounces of BBs inside. This suruchin is in the style of the Kashaka, an African musical instrument created from two gourds filled with beans. This creates a distinctive sound while casting during kata performance.

Figure 54 Traditional Kashaka; photozou: Ludwig D. Omen, CC BY 2.1 JP, via Wikimedia Commons

53

Practice Suruchin

The following photos depict five different styles of practice suruchin (a very wise investment when starting out):

1. A monkey fist suruchin using 750 paracord and ¾" steel ball bearings. Weights are too small for use as a weapon, but very compact for travel.
2. A tennis ball suruchin using 550 paracord and 2" tennis balls (such as those used for pet toys). Holes are drilled in the tennis balls, and the rope pushed through with a "paracord needle." The rope is finished with an Ashley stopper knot (ABoK #526). This is by far the best kind of practice suruchin for the beginning practitioner.
3. A child-size monkey fist suruchin using soft cotton rope and a wooden bead as the core.
4. A full-size tennis ball connected to cotton 3/8" rope. A PVC pipe with drilled & glued caps is added for a handle (stained for appearance).
5. A fishing weight (south bend bank sinkers) wrapped with tape, attached to 550 paracord; good for full-contact practice against a Kobudo dummy (wooden post wrapped in rope)

Figure 55 3/4" ball bearing suruchin

Figure 56 Tennis ball suruchin

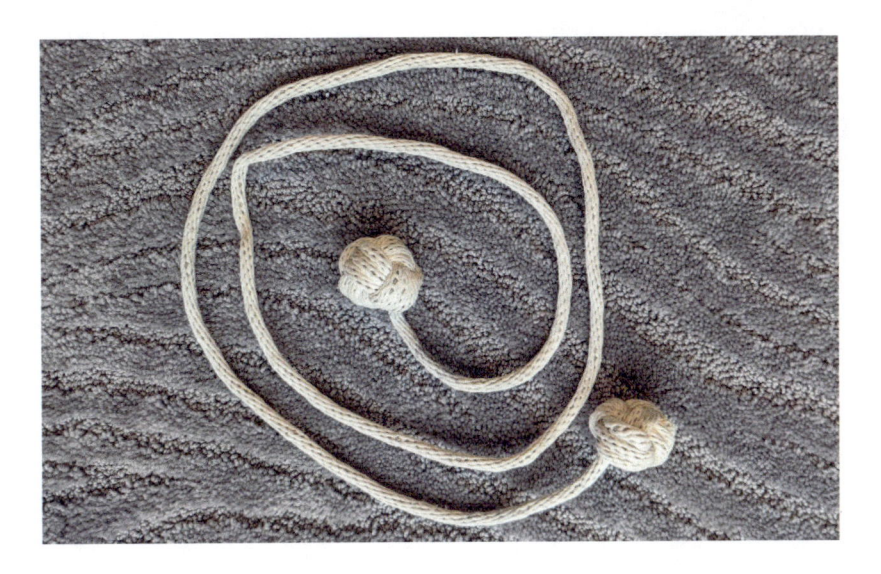

Figure 57 Cotton rope/wooden bead suruchin

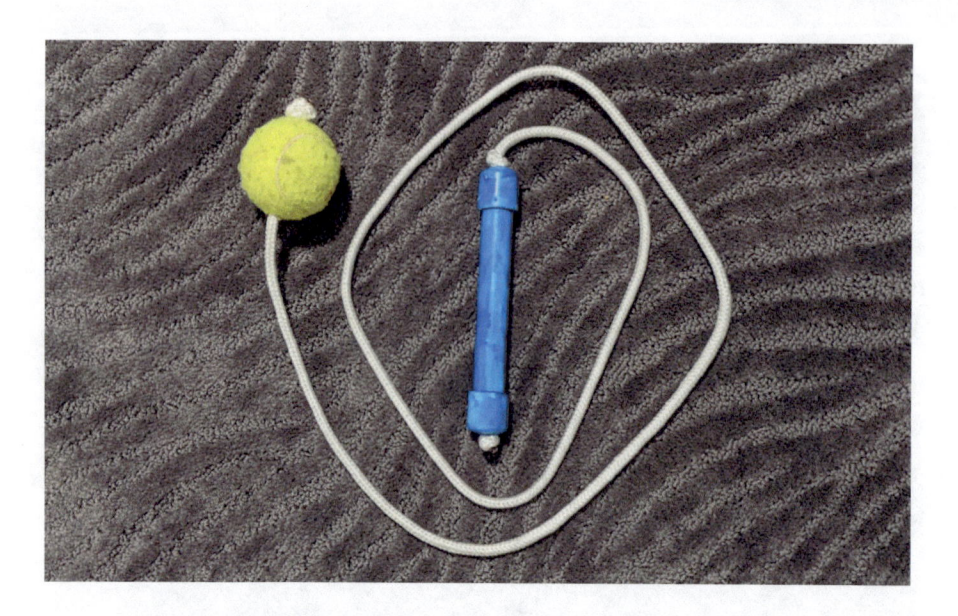

Figure 58 Handle-type practice short suruchin

Figure 59 Fishing weight suruchin

Constructing a Pocket Suruchin

Figure 60 Pocket Suruchin (collapsed)

Figure 61 Pocket suruchin (expanded)

This section will discuss the construction of a concealed pocket suruchin, the invention of the author. This suruchin has the advantage that, in its concealed form, it can double as a Yawara or Kubaton weapon before being deployed.

IMPORTANT NOTE ON ROPE STRENGTH:

Manufacturers will commonly list a rope's breaking (or tensile) strength. This value is very different from a rope's safe working load; a rope's breaking strength is tested under ideal conditions in a laboratory on brand new rope with no wear, with the ropes wrapped around drums and subjected to slowly increasing stress until breaking point is reached. Knots will typically introduce a weak point, reducing rope strength by 10-40%. In addition, a 100lb load on a rope that is jerked around will put a stress on the rope far higher than 100lb. A general rule of thumb is that the safe working load for a rope is 20% of the breaking strength. So, to swing a rope with a 1/2lb weight on the end (without hitting anything) would produce around 2.5lb of force on the rope, so you would need a rope with at least 12.5lbs breaking strength. However, to wrap/trap and throw a 200lb opponent, you would want a rope with at least 1,000lbs breaking strength. Case in point, a length of 550lb of paracord will snap in half if attempting to use as a climbing rope for a 100lb child (personal experience from the author's childhood). Ideally, even for a practice suruchin with tennis balls the author would not use a rope with less than 50lb breaking strength for safety.

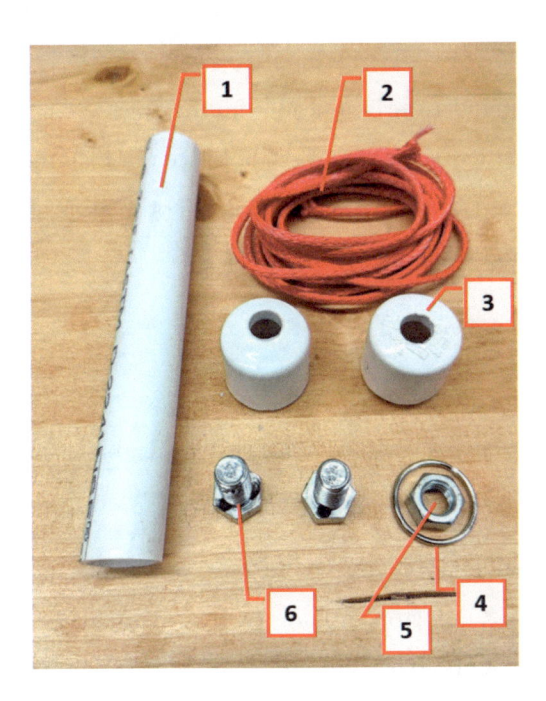

Figure 62 Pocket suruchin parts list

Parts list:

1. 5" long ½" SDR-13.5, 315PSI PVC pipe or equivalent (note: it is important to get this and not schedule 40 PVC pipe, which due to the thicker wall has too little space inside for the rope)

2. Appropriate length rope (1.5 times arm span; see suruchin measurement section). The rope used here was 3/32" HTS-99 from mapleleafropes.com, with a breaking strength of 2000lb (material: Dyneema® SK99).

3. 2x ½" PVC pie caps, with 3/8" holes drilled in the ends

4. 1x Keyring; there are titanium ones available that are much more durable that standard keyrings

5. 1x 3/8" nut

6. 2x 3/8"x1/2" bolts. These are modified; each bolt has two 5/32" holes drilled at a 45-degree angle just under the bolt head, with the holes meeting in a single exit hole in the center of the top of the bolt (see photos). In addition, one of the bolts has an extra 1/8" hole drilled in the end of the bolt. A vise and drill press are ideal for modifying these bolts.

Construction:

After all parts are modified as described in the parts' list, you can color the PVC as desired by using 1mL of solvent (or petroleum dye such as Rekhaoil Red HF, etc.) in a 4oz can of PVC clear cleaner.

First thread the rope through the middle of the head of the bolt, wrap halfway around, back down the other hole, and tie a stopper knot (such as the Ashley Stopper, ABoK #526) as shown in the photo. Repeat on the other end of the rope.

For the back end ("A"), insert the bolt without the additional hole and tighten the nut on the other end. A drop of glue/epoxy will help ensure this nut never comes off. Then slide the 5" PVC pipe over the rope and use PVC cement to permanently lock it into the cap.

For the front end ("B"), insert the second bolt through the other cap. Secure bolt by placing keyring through hole in end of bolt. This cap end WILL NOT be glued in place.

Finish off with a handful of keys for weight. About a dozen does well. For practice suruchins, sometimes hardware stores or locksmiths will have a box of mis-cut or throwaway keys you can get for free. If keys are not providing enough weight, the "Bank Sinkers" fishing weights (available form 2-8oz) can be easily added.

Lastly, it works well to wrap the rope around your hand as shown in the photo, then take the rope off your hand and slide into the tube as a bundle. This helps avoid snagging.

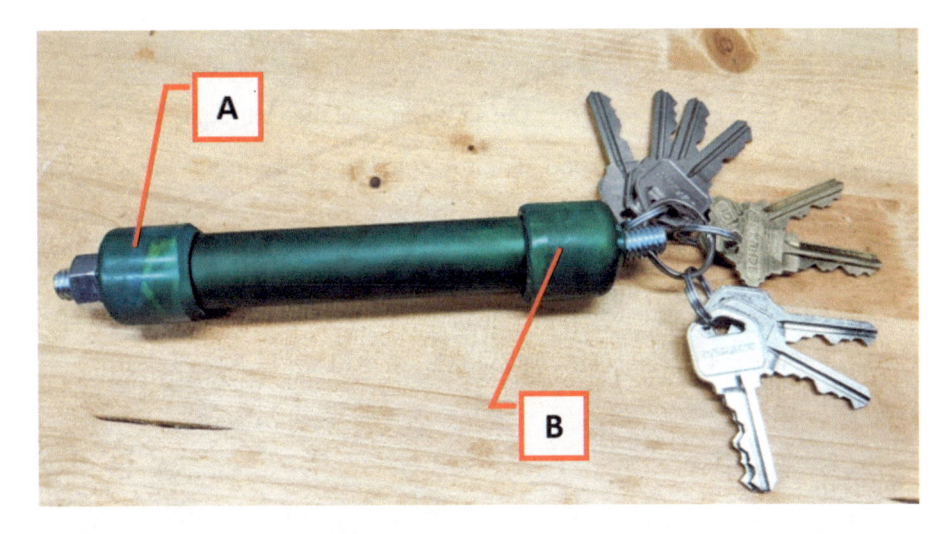

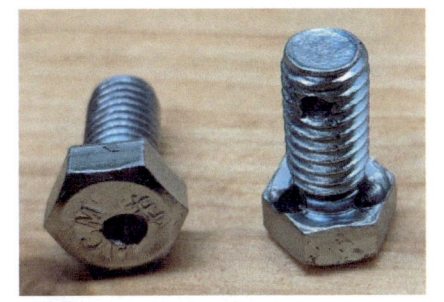

Figure 63 Construction of pocket suruchin

Figure 64 Wrapping for storage

61

Hojōjutsu (Tying and Binding)

The techniques of Hojōjutsu, or the Japanese martial art of tying and restraining opponents with rope, are not traditional to the suruchin weapon. However, it is so closely related to the suruchin, and the techniques lend themselves so well to the weapon, that a section is included in this book to help the practitioner realize the full potential of the suruchin in training. This is a full martial art in and of itself, so this section does not attempt to fully explore all possibilities. A few representative techniques are shown; there are excellent resources [15,16,17] available to the student who wishes to learn more.

Figure 65 Captive prisoner before magistrate, 1870 by Shimooka Renjō

Figure 66 Japanese prisoner, late 1800's

Brief History of Hojōjutsu

While tying up an enemy with rope goes as far back in history as rope itself, the first recording of Japanese Hojōjutsu techniques dates to approximately 1467. Originally for the Bushi class, this art became one of the "18 Warrior's Skills" (along with archery, horseback riding, etc.). However, it was during the Edo period (1603-1868) that the art truly came into its own.

The rope was used by police officers before the advent of modern handcuffs to detain and transport criminals. They would hold down a criminal using joint locks, and then dispense rope from a small bundle held in the hand as they wrapped limbs and neck. The actual workings of the techniques of various schools were kept secret as much as possible (in part to help keep criminals from circumventing the knots). There are literally hundreds of techniques, and separate knots were used to denote both the type of prisoner (Samurai, Monk, farmer, women, children, etc.) as well as whether the crime committed was a minor or major offense. In addition, the color of the rope had significance; white, yellow, red, blue or black could signify the Guardians of Chinese Taoism (as a talisman against negative energies), the elements, the seasons, or (later) the precinct that made the arrest.

Figure 67 Seiko Fujita, Zukai Torinawajutsu author 1898 – 1966

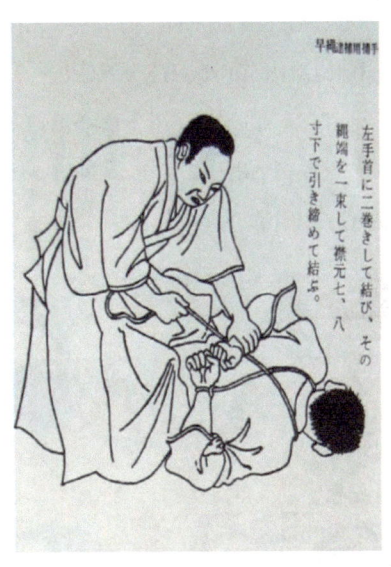

Figure 68 Capturing technique, from Zukai Torinawajutsu

The Techniques of Hojōjutsu

Hojōjutsu has two main categories of techniques; first is Hayanawa (fast rope), which is for the initial arrest of a criminal. It uses simpler, straightforward, and fast techniques using a slender (3-4mm) rope of approximately 4.5-6.5 meters in length (though sometimes 2 meters, depending on the school) with a small loop in one end, and was meant for a resisting opponent. The techniques on the following pages using the suruchin are Hayanawa techniques.

The second category uses Honnawa (main rope) techniques. These would typically be used in the transportation of prisoners, and would be far more elaborate and detailed, and customized to the category of prisoner. The ropes used would be 6-8mm thick, and anywhere from 6.5-20 meters long.

Rope coil

This small rope bundle (or Hojōmaki) allowed rope to be dispensed from one end without tangling during an arrest. It also allows for a method of storing a suruchin so that it can be carried in a gear bag without becoming tangled throughout the bag and allows for rapid deployment of the suruchin when ready. A slight modification is made from the original method since there is a weight on both ends; it ends in a slip knot instead of going completely through the loop.

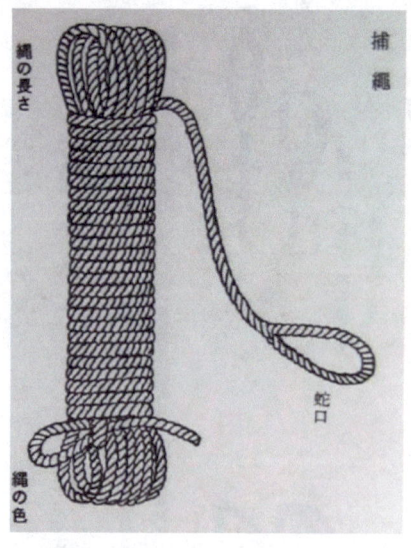

Figure 69 Rope coil, from Zukai Torinawajutsu

1. Hold one end in hand, with thumb and forefinger extended

2. Wrap rope around fingers in figure 8 pattern, leaving about 16"

3. Wrap coil with remaining rope, finish with slipped loop (pull bottom weight to secure slipped loop)

4 Knots

The four simple knots detailed on the following pages are a tiny sampling of what is possible with the suruchin.

Jaguchi (end loop) slip knot, for the initial loop around wrist or neck; pinch rope through splice and pull through

65

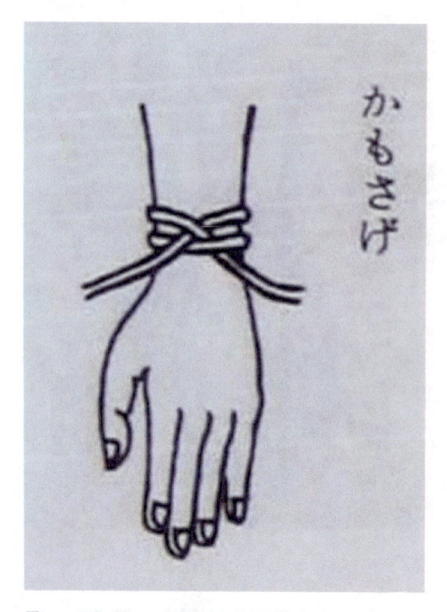

Figure 70 Kamagakushi, from Zukai Torinawajutsu

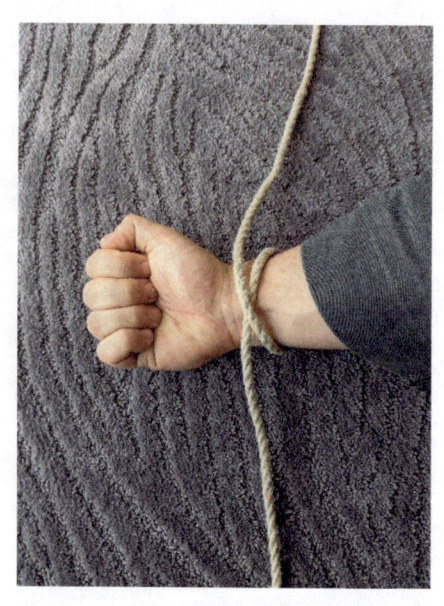

1. Wrap around wrist (or wrists)

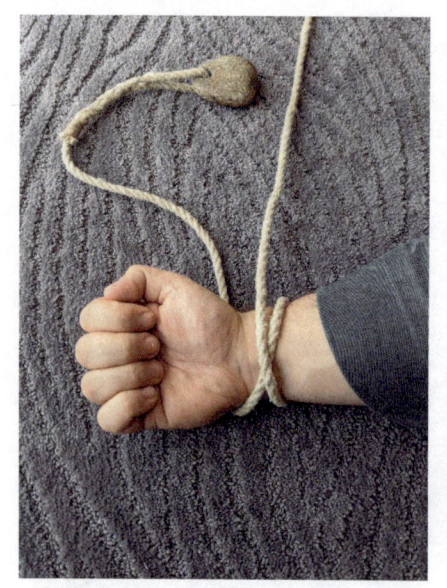

2. Continue wrapping

3. Pass on same side of standing end as loop, pass under first loop

Kamagakushi (or Sack knot, ABoK #1243) Good for binding wrists together.

66

1. Wrap around first two fingers (spread out) 3 times

2. Feed both ends back through the 3 loops

3. Pull loops tight; tighten on wrists by pulling loose ends

Tejo Nawa (or Handcuff knot, or Commercial Cord Curtain Holdback, ABoK #1113) There is a slightly simpler handcuff knot (Kake-musubi, or ABoK #1134), but this one is more secure.

1. With rope draped over wrist, grab one side (can be either side)

2. Bend hand down and pinch other side with 1st and 2nd fingers

3. Allow loop around wrist to fall off over fingers

4. Pull/shake to enlarge loop

Kata-Musubi (Or Slip knot, ABoK #529) A fast one-handed slipping loop that can be formed while the other hand is holding the rest of the line tight.

68

Hayanawa technique – Variant 1

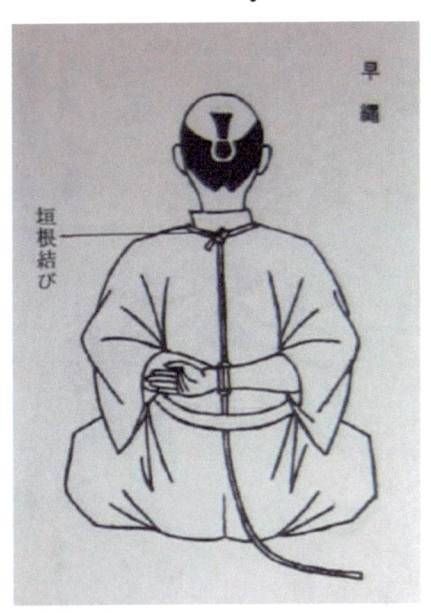

Figure 71 Hayanawa technique 1, from Zukai Torinawajutsu [16]

1. Pinch rope through splice and pull through to make slip knot

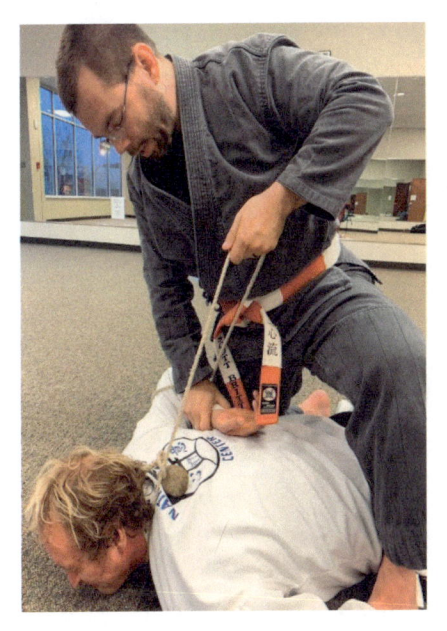

2. Loop slip knot around neck

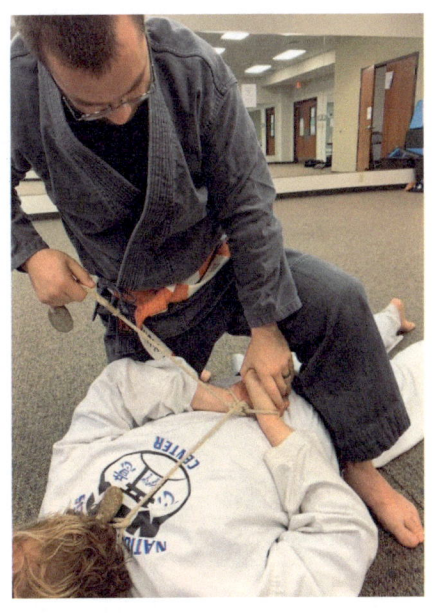

3. Bind both wrists with Tejo Nawa (shown) or Kamagakushi; finish with overhand knot as desired

Hayanawa technique – Variant 2

Figure 72 Hayanawa technique 2, from Zukai Torinawajutsu [16]

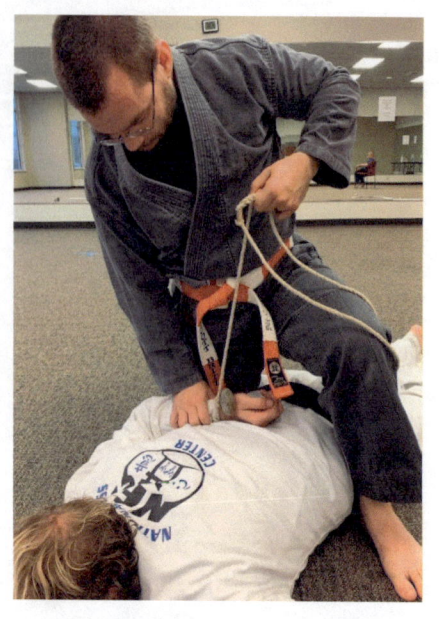

1. Make slip knot similar to step 1 of Hayanawa 1 technique; bind R wrist

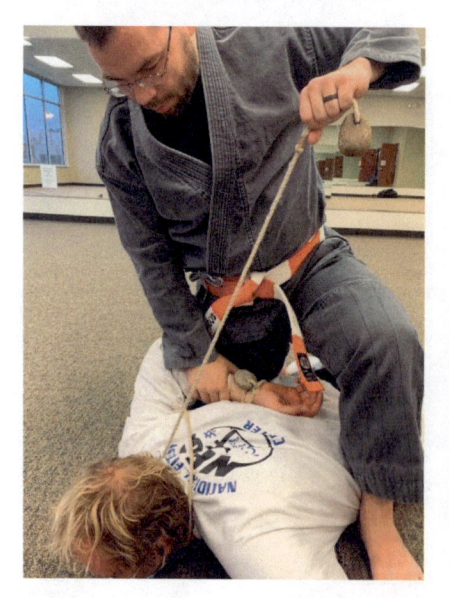

2. Thread rope around opposite side of neck

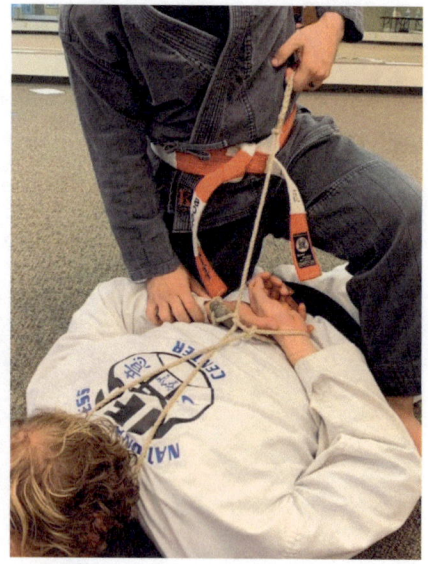

3. Bind left wrist with Kata-Musubi, overhand knot to right wrist, or bind both wrists with Kamagakushi

Suruchin Techniques

Techniques key

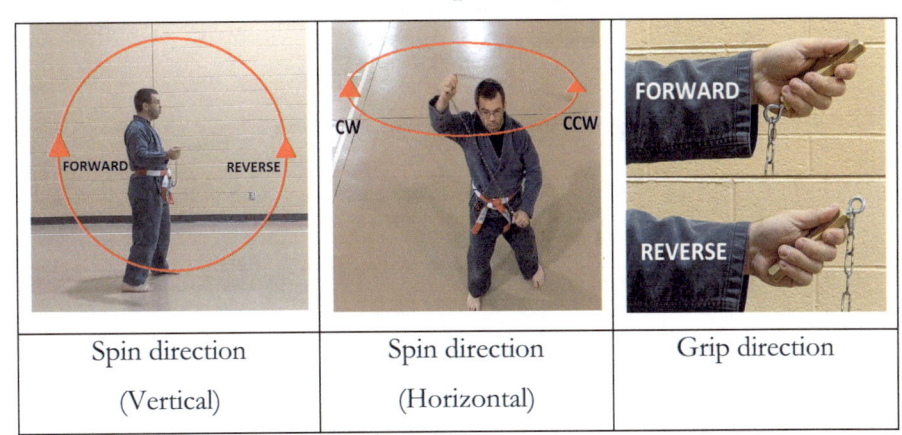

Spin direction (Vertical)	Spin direction (Horizontal)	Grip direction

General suruchin abbreviations:

FW =	Forward	H =	Holds	B =	Blocks
RV =	Reverse	S =	Swings	ST =	Stretch
CW =	Clockwise	C =	Cast/Strike	SH =	Shorten
CC =	Counterclockwise				

Movement Abbreviations:

RFF =	Right foot forward	LFF =	Left foot forward
RFB =	Right foot back	LFB =	Left foot back
RS =	Right Side	LS =	Left Side
ST =	Straight		

The following techniques list is in alphabetical order by abbreviation.

#	Abbreviation	Description	Page
\multicolumn{4}{c}{Holds}			
1	H.BLT.RS	Wear suruchin as belt, weights to right side	64
2	H.CHG.LH	Change hands, handle in left hand, weight in right	64
3	H.CHG.RH	Change hands, handle in right hand, weight in left	65
4	H.DBF.FW	Double hand hold, chain folded, handle forward	66
5	H.DBF.RV	Double hand hold, chain folded, handle reversed	66
6	H.FLD.DB	Folded in thirds in both hands, manriki length	67
7	H.GTH.LH	Gathered in left hand, weight in right hand	68
8	H.GTH.RH	Gathered hold in right hand	68
9	H.LHE.FW	Left hand extended hold, handle forward	68
10	H.LHE.RV	Left hand extended hold, handle reversed	69
11	H.LHG.FW	Left hand gathered hold, handle forward	69
12	H.LHG.RV	Left hand gathered hold, handle reversed	69
13	H.RHG.FW	Right hand grip (chain only over hand)	70
14	H.STD.FW	Standard hold (handle in left hand, middle of chain in right hand), chain forward	70
15	H.STD.RV	Standard hold (handle in left hand, middle of chain in right hand), chain reversed	70
16	H.SWH.FW	Switch handle direction to forwards	71
17	H.SWH.RV	Switch handle direction to reverse	71
18	H.WDB.RH	Wrap doubled Chain/rope around right hand	71
19	H.WRP.RH	Wrap Chain/rope around right hand to shorten	72

Swings

20	S.BCK.CW	Transfer suruchin around back, clockwise	73
21	S.CAT.LH	Catch swinging weight with left hand, ending with doubled hold	74
22	S.CHG.HT	Change direction by letting weight hit ground	74
23	S.CHG.ST	Change direction by stalling in air	75
24	S.DBL.F8	Figure 8 pattern with both weights at once	76
25	S.DBL.FW	Swing both weights forwards	76
26	S.DBL.RV	Swing both weights in opposite directions	77
27	S.ELB.FW	Catch on elbow (change direction), forward swing	77
28	S.ELB.RV	Catch on elbow (change direction), reverse swing	78
29	S.EXT.CC	Fully extended overhead swing, counterclockwise	79
30	S.EXT.CW	Fully extended overhead swing, clockwise	79
31	S.EXT.F8	Fully extended figure 8 swing	80
32	S.FG8.FW	Swing figure of 8, forward direction	80
33	S.FG8.RV	Swing figure of 8, reverse direction	80
34	S.FRT.CC	Swing in front, counterclockwise direction	81
35	S.FRT.CW	Swing in front, clockwise direction	81
36	S.HD8.FW	Figure-8 swing with suruchin handle, forwards	81
37	S.HD8.RV	Figure-8 swing with suruchin handle, reverse	82
38	S.LSD.FW	Swing at left side, forward direction	82
39	S.LSD.RV	Swing at left side, reverse direction	82
40	S.OVH.CC	Swing overhead, counterclockwise direction	83
41	S.OVH.CW	Swing overhead, clockwise direction	83
42	S.RSD.FW	Swing at right side, forward direction	83
43	S.RSD.RV	Swing at right side, reverse direction	84

Casting / Strikes

44	C.DBL.LS	Double strike (both weights) to left side	85
45	C.DBL.RS	Double strike (both weights) to right side	85
46	C.DBS.LS	Double weight swing to left side	87
47	C.DBS.RS	Double weight swing to right side	87
48	C.DNC.LS	Downward cast, 45 degrees from left side	87
49	C.DNC.RS	Downward cast, 45 degrees from right side	88
50	C.DNC.ST	Downward cast, straight down	88
51	C.DNS.LS	Downward strike, 45 degrees from left side	88
52	C.DNS.RS	Downward strike, 45 degrees from right side	89
53	C.DNS.ST	Downward strike, straight down	89
54	C.ELB.LS	Elbow cast, left side	89
55	C.ELB.RS	Elbow cast, right side	90
56	C.FOT.FW	Cast with right foot forward direction	90
57	C.FOT.LS	Cast with right foot to the left	91
58	C.FOT.MD	Cast with right foot forward, modified (looping)	91
59	C.HDL.FW	Strike with handle, forward grip	92
60	C.HDL.RV	Strike with handle, reverse grip	92
61	C.HKN.RS	Horizontal swing at right side while kneeling	93
62	C.HZC.LS	Horizontal cast at left side	93
63	C.HZC.RS	Horizontal cast at right side	93
64	C.HZS.LS	Horizontal swing at left side	94
65	C.HZS.RS	Horizontal swing at right side	94
66	C.KNE.LS	Knee cast, left side	94
67	C.KNE.RS	Knee cast, right side	95
68	C.ROP.DB	Strike with both weights in 1 hand, rope end	95
69	C.UP4.LS	Upward cast, 45 degrees from left side	95
70	C.UP4.RS	Upward cast, 45 degrees from right side	96

71	C.UPC.BK	Upward cast to the backward direction	96
72	C.UPC.LS	Upward cast to the left side	96
73	C.UPC.RS	Upward cast to the right side	97
74	C.UPC.ST	Upward cast, straight up	97
75	C.UPS.LS	Upward strike, 45 degrees from left side	97
76	C.UPS.RS	Upward strike, 45 degrees from right side	98
77	C.UPS.ST	Upward strike, straight up	98
78	C.WGT.1W	Strike with one weight held in thumb/forefinger	98
79	C.WGT.DB	Strike with both weights held in hand	99
80	C.WRP.RS	Cast weight while wrapped around right hand	99

Blocks

81	B.CHN.LS	Check with doubled chain to left side	100
82	B.CHN.RS	Check with doubled chain to right side	100
83	B.DBH.LS	Double block high to the left side	100
84	B.DBH.RS	Double block high to the right side	101
85	B.DBL.RH	Double block to the right side	101
86	B.DBL.LH	Double block to the left side	101
87	B.DBR.LW	Double block Low	102
88	B.DBR.OH	Double block overhead	102
89	B.LCH.LS	Leg check (swing handle down) to the left side	102
90	B.LCH.RS	Leg check (swing weight down) to the right side	103
91	B.NCH.LS	Nunchuck block, left side	103
92	B.NCH.RS	Nunchuck block, right side	103
93	B.VTL.RH	Vertical block to the left, right hand high	104
94	B.VTR.LH	Vertical block to the right, left hand high	104

Holds

1. H.BLT.RS   Belt hold

Wear suruchin as belt, weights to right side

2.a H.CHG.LH   Change hands (left)

Handle in right hand, weight in left

2.b

Move first finger of right hand to other side of handle, pinch weight

Holds

2.c

Take handle in left hand

3.a H.CHG.RH   Change hands (right)

Handle in left hand, weight in right

3.b

Move first finger of left hand to other side of handle, pinch weight

Holds

3.c

Take handle in right hand

4. H.DBF.FW   Doubled hold (forward)

Double hand hold, chain folded, handle forward

5. H.DBF.RV   Doubled hold (reverse)

Double hand hold, chain folded, handle reversed

Holds

6.a H.FLD.DB Folded in thirds

Hold both ends in reverse hold

6.b

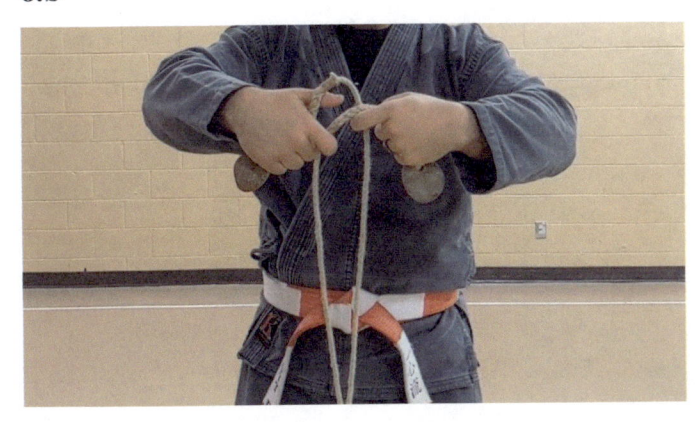

Hook first finger of both hands on opposite side's rope

6.c

Pull out to create a three-strand rope

Holds

7. H.GTH.LH Gathered (left)

Gathered hold in left hand, with weight in right hand (4-8" out)

8. H.GTH.RH Gathered (right)

Gathered hold in right hand (usually transferred from gathered in left hand, before bowing out)

9. H.LHE.FW Left hand extended (forward)

Left hand extended hold, handle forward

Holds

10. H.LHE.RV Left hand extended (reverse)

Left hand extended hold, handle reversed

11. H.LHG.FW Left hand gathered (forward)

Left hand gathered hold, handle forward

12. H.LHG.RV Left hand gathered (reverse)

Left hand gathered hold, handle reversed

Holds

13. H.RHG.FW Right hand grip

Right hand grip (chain only over hand)

14. H.STD.FW Standard hold (forward)

Standard hold (handle in left hand, middle of chain in right hand), chain forward (away from thumb)

15. H.STD.RV Standard hold (reverse)

Standard hold (handle in left hand, middle of chain in right hand), chain reversed (towards thumb)

Holds

16. H.SWH.FW   Switch handle (forward)

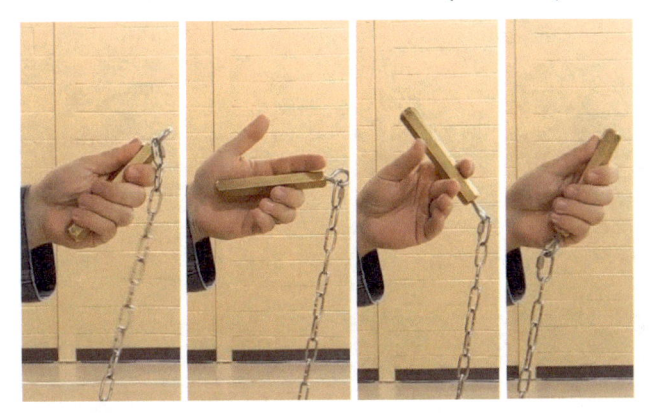

Switch handle from reverse to forwards grip

17. H.SWH.RV   Switch handle (reverse)

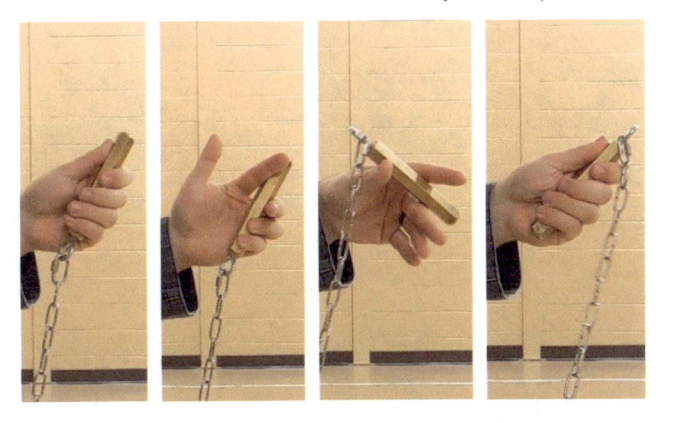

Switch handle from forwards to reverse grip

18. H.WDB.RH   Wrap doubled chain

Wrap middle of rope around right hand (stick pinky in midpoint of loop)

19. H.WRP.RH Wrap chain

Wrap Chain/rope around right hand to shorten

Swings

20.a S.BCK.CW   Transfer around back

Transfer suruchin around back, clockwise; start with extended swing

20.b

Pass behind back, transfer handle to left hand

20.c

Continue swing and catch middle of rope with right hand

Swings

21. S.CAT.LH Catch weight

Catch swinging weight (counter-clockwise) in left hand

22.a S.CHG.HT Change direction; hit

Change directions by allowing weight to hit ground; start with forward swing

22.b

Allow weight to hit ground to stop

Swings

22.c

Pull and start swing in opposite direction

23.a S.CHG.ST   Change direction; stall

Change directions by stalling in mid-air; applicable to all swing directions

23.b

Suddenly extend hand in direction of taught rope to stall circular motion

Swings

23.c

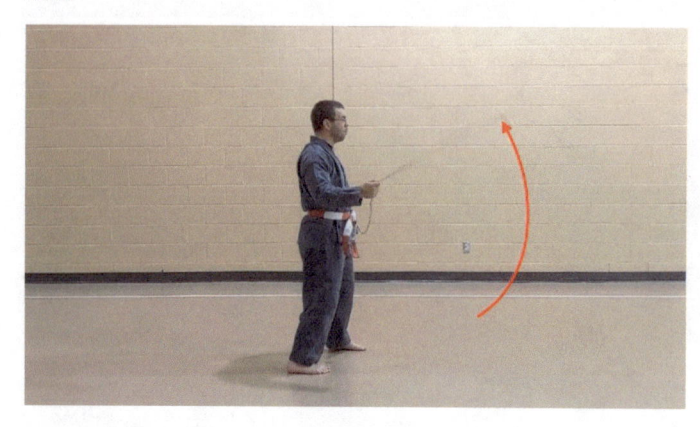

Pull and start swing in opposite direction

24. S.DBL.F8   Double figure 8

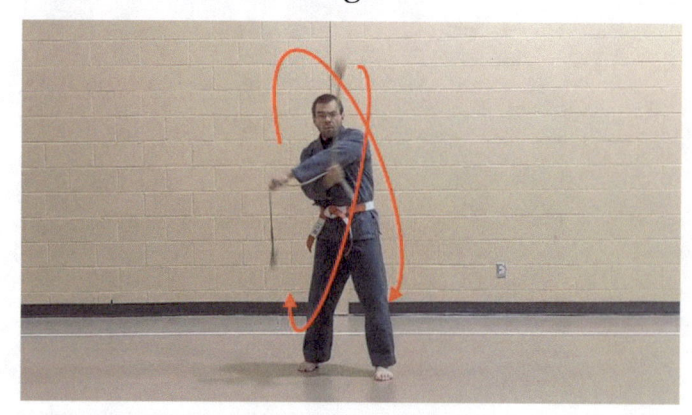

Figure 8 pattern with both weights at once

25. S.DBL.FW   Double forwards

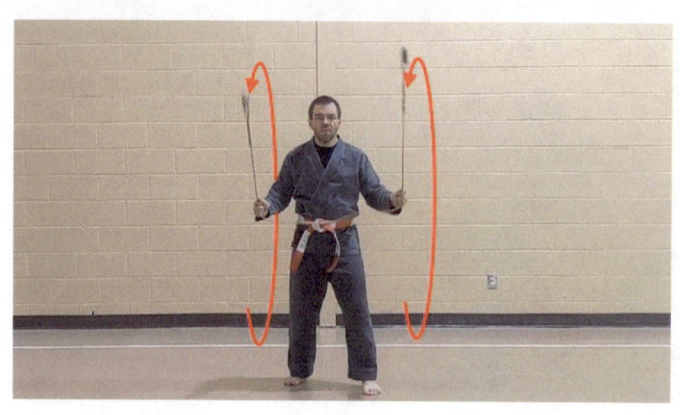

Swing both weights forwards

Swings

26. S.DBL.RV   Double swing, opposite

Swing both weights in opposite directions

27.a S.ELB.FW   Change direction on elbow; FW

Catch on elbow (change direction), forward swing. Swing at right side, forwards

27.b

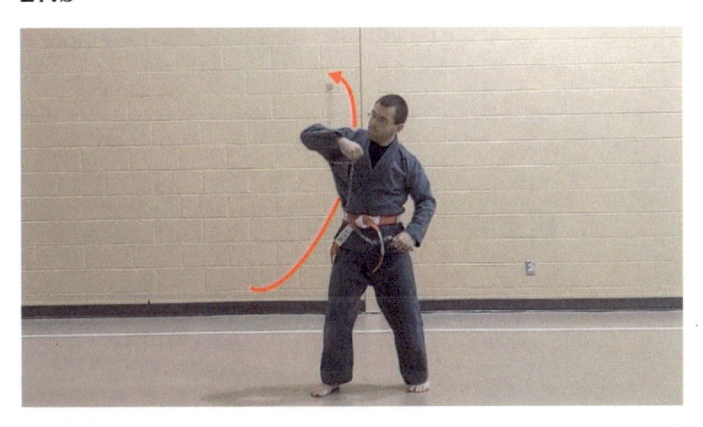

Extend right elbow out to catch chain

89

Swings

27.c

Pivot feet to turn other direction, using elbow to move trajectory of suruchin to other side

28.a S.ELB.RV   Change direction on elbow; RV

Catch on elbow (change direction), reverse swing. Extend right elbow out to catch chain

28.b

Move elbow to the right (behind) to move trajectory to other side while…

Swings

28.c

...Pivoting feet to face other direction

29. S.EXT.CC   Extended overhead, CC

Fully extended swing overheard, counter-clockwise direction

30. S.EXT.CW   Extended overhead, CW

Fully extended swing overheard, clockwise direction

Swings

31. S.EXT.F8   Extended figure 8

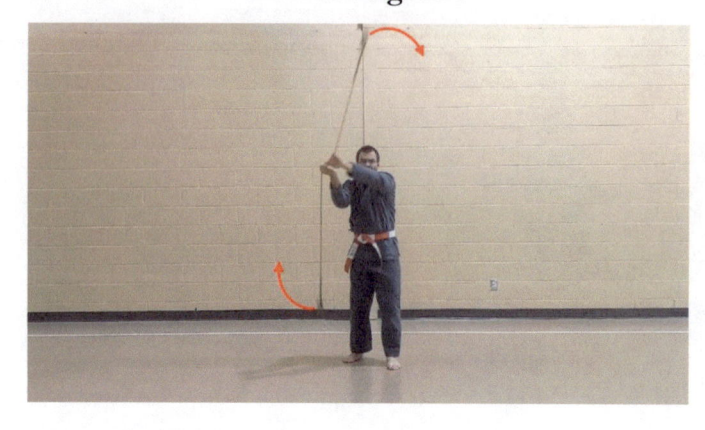

Fully extended figure 8 swing (start with S.DBL.F8 and slowly bring hands together)

32. S.FG8.FW   Figure 8 (forward)

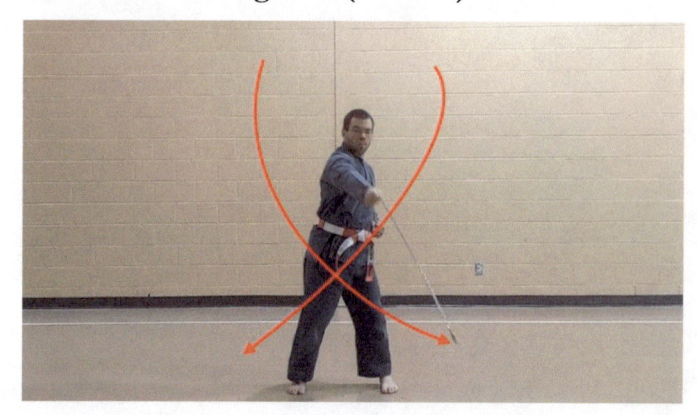

Swing figure of 8, forward direction

33. S.FG8.RV   Figure 8 (reverse)

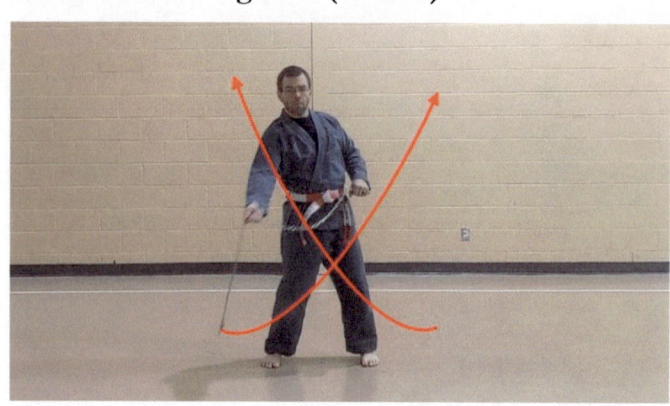

Swing figure of 8, reverse direction

Swings

34. S.FRT.CC   Circle at front CC

Swing in front, counterclockwise direction

35. S.FRT.CW   Circle at front CW

Swing in front, clockwise direction

36. S.HD8.FW   Figure 8 with handle (forward)

Figure-8 swing with suruchin handle, forwards

Swings

37. S.HD8.RV   Figure 8 with handle (reverse)

Figure-8 swing with suruchin handle, reverse

38. S.LSD.FW   Left side (forward)

Swing at left side, forward direction

39. S.LSD.RV   Left side (reverse)

Swing at left side, reverse direction

40. S.OVH.CC   Overhead, CC

Swing overhead, counter-clockwise direction

41. S.OVH.CW   Overhead, CW

Swing overhead, clockwise direction

42. S.RSD.FW   Right side (forward)

Swing at right side, forward direction

Swings

43. S.RSD.RV Right side (reverse)

Swing at right side, reverse direction

Casting/Strikes

44. C.DBL.LS   Double strike, left

Double strike (both weights) to left side. Reverse steps of C.DBL.RS, from Part e to Part a

45.a C.DBL.RS   Double strike, right

Double strike (both weights) to right side. Starting with weights wrapped from left side swing.

45.b

Swing both weights horizontally towards front

Casting/Strikes

45.c

Continue swing around and over head

45.d

Continue swing down to right side (weight in right hand is now on top)

45.e

Allow swing to wrap around body

Casting/Strikes

46. C.DBS.LS Doubled swing, left

Holding middle of doubled rope H.WDB.RH swing to left side

47. C.DBS.RS Doubled swing, right

Holding middle of doubled rope H.WDB.RH swing to right side

48. C.DNC.LS Downward cast, left

Downward cast, 45 degrees from left side

Casting/Strikes

49. C.DNC.RS   Downward cast, right

Downward cast, 45 degrees from right side

50. C.DNC.ST   Downward cast, straight

Downward cast, straight down

51. C.DNS.LS   Downward swing, left

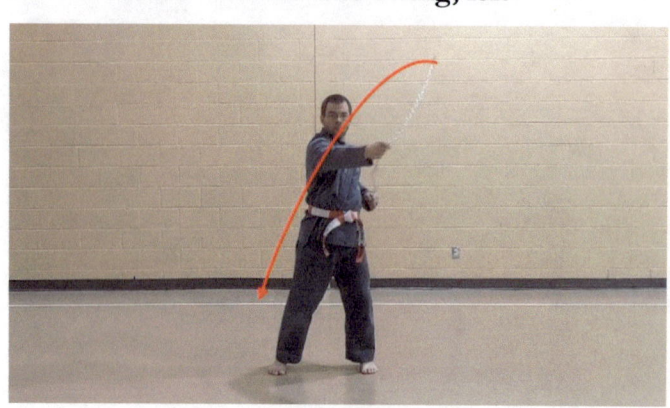

Downward strike, 45 degrees from left side

Casting/Strikes

52. C.DNS.RS Downward swing, right

Downward strike, 45 degrees from right side

53. C.DNS.ST Downward swing, straight

Downward strike, straight down

54. C.ELB.LS Elbow cast, left

Swing forwards at left side, allow to wrap left elbow and slip off to cast backward (see C.ELB.RS)

Casting/Strikes

55. C.ELB.RS Elbow cast, right

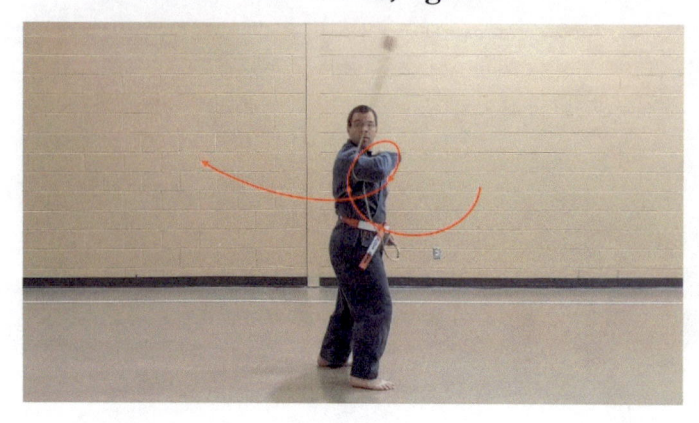

Swing forwards at right side, allow to wrap right elbow and slip off to cast backward

56.a C.FOT.FW Foot cast, foward

Cast with right foot forward direction. Forward swing…

56.b

Catch last 3-4 inches on outward turned right foot

Casting/Strikes

56.c

Kick out with right foot, sending weight forward (side view)

57. C.FOT.LS   Foot cast, left

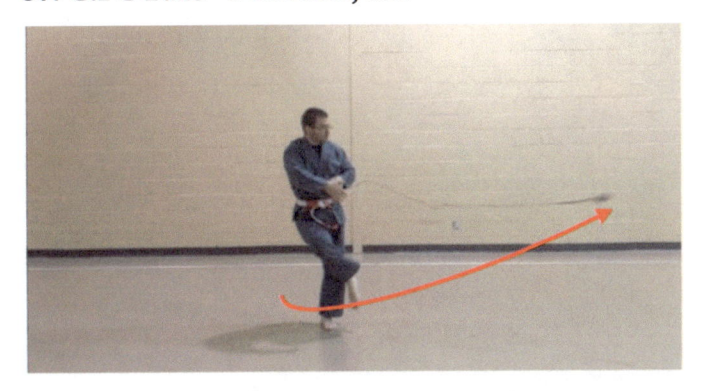

Cast with right foot to the left. Same as C.FOT.FW except in Part c, kick to left

58.a C.FOT.MD   Modified foot cast

Cast with right foot forward, modified (looping). Forward swing

103

Casting/Strikes

58.b

Catch last 1-1.5ft of rope on outturned right foot, allow to swing in tight loop outside of leg to cast

59. C.HDL.FW   Handle thrust, forward

Forward thrusting strike with butt of handle

60. C.HDL.RV   Handle thrust, reverse

Thrusting strike with chain end of handle, or hammer fist strike with butt of handle

Casting/Strikes

61. C.HKN.RS   Horizontal kneeling strike

Horizontal cast at right side while kneeling

62. C.HZC.LS   Horizontal cast, left

Horizontal cast at left side

63. C.HZC.RS   Horizontal cast, right

Horizontal cast at right side

Casting/Strikes

64. C.HZS.LS Horizontal swing, left

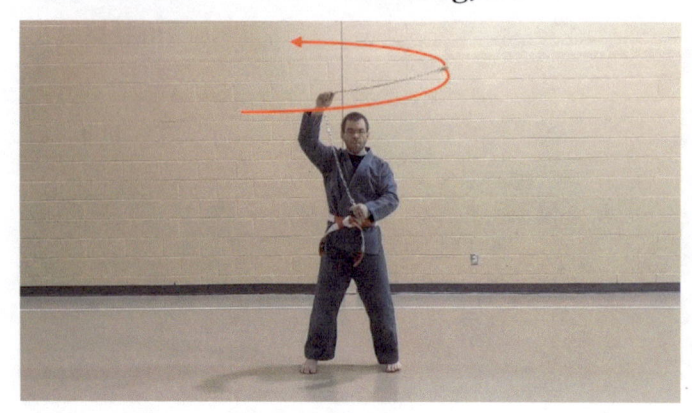

Horizontal swing at left side

65. C.HZS.RS Horizontal swing, right

Horizontal swing at right side

66. C.KNE.LS Knee cast, left

Left side knee cast; forward swing; allow to wrap right knee and slip off to cast forwards

Casting/Strikes

67. C.KNE.RS Knee cast, right

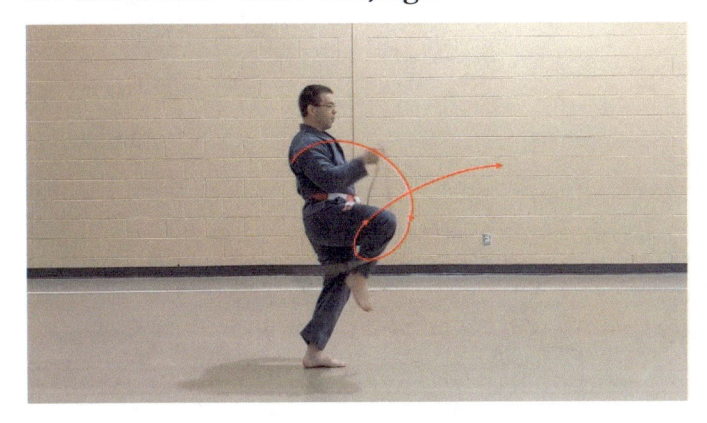

Right side knee cast; forward swing; allow to wrap right knee and slip off to cast forwards

68. C.ROP.DB Strike with doubled rope

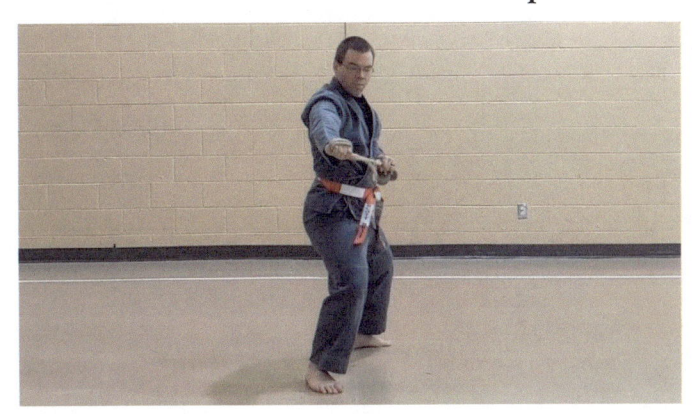

From H.WDB.RH, strike with rope-wrapped right hand

69. C.UP4.LS Upward cast, left 45

Upward cast, 45 degrees from left side

Casting/Strikes

70. C.UP4.RS   Upward cast, right 45

Upward cast, 45 degrees from right side

71. C.UPC.BK   Upward cast, back

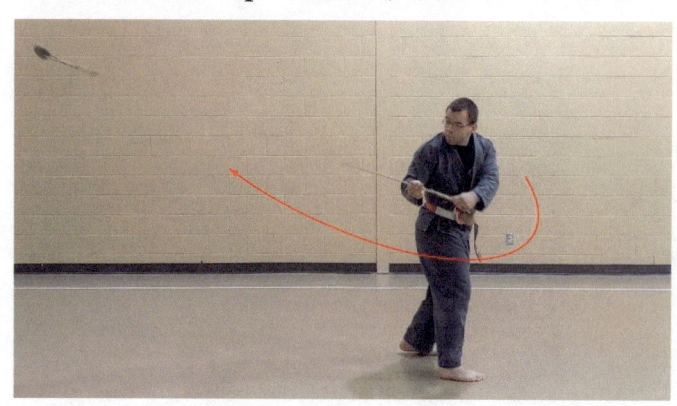

Upward cast to the back, starting with forward swing at right side

72. C.UPC.LS   Upward cast, left side

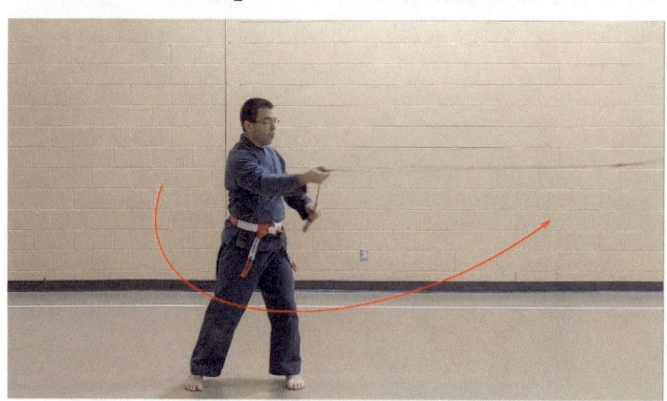

Starting with front circle S.FRT.CW, cast to left side

Casting/Strikes

73. C.UPC.RS Upward cast, right side

Starting with front circle S.FRT.CC, cast to right side

74. C.UPC.ST Upward cast, straight

Upward cast, straight up

75. C.UPS.LS Upward strike, left 45

Upward strike, 45 degrees from left side

Casting/Strikes

76. C.UPS.RS Upward strike, right 45

Upward strike, 45 degrees from right side

77. C.UPS.ST Upward strike, straight

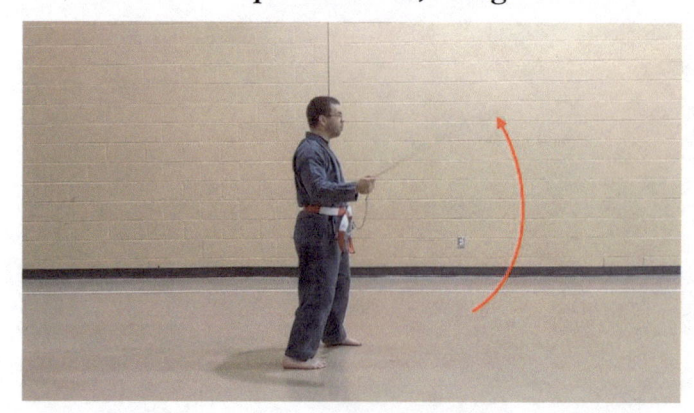

Upward strike, straight up

78. C.WGT.1W Strike with weight

Thrusting strike with weight held in thumb/ forefinger grip

Casting/Strikes

79. C.WGT.DB   Strike with both weights

From H.WDB.RH, strike with double weights

80. C.WRP.RS   Cast wrapped weight

With rope around right hand (H.WRP.RH) upward cast, right fingers extended straight to allow coiled rope to release

111

Blocks

81. B.CHN.LS   Chain parry, left

Check (parry) with doubled chain to left side

82. B.CHN.RS   Chain parry, right

Check (parry) with doubled chain to right side

83. B.DBH.LS   Double block, left

Doubled block to the left, right hand high

Blocks

84. B.DBH.RS   Double block, right

Doubled block to the right, left hand high

85. B.DBL.RH   Double high block, right

Doubled high block to the right side

86. B.DBL.LH   Double high block, left

Doubled high block to the left side

113

Blocks

87. B.DBR.LW   Double block, low

Double block
Low

88. B.DBR.OH   Double block, overhead

Double block
overhead

89. B.LCH.LS   Leg check, left

Leg check
(swing weight
down) to the
left side (use
handle)

Blocks

90. B.LCH.RS Leg check, right

Leg check (swing weight down) to the right side

91. B.NCH.LS Nunchuck block, left

Nunchuck block, left side with suruchin doubled

92. B.NCH.RS Nunchuck block, right

Nunchuck block, right side with suruchin doubled

115

Blocks

93. B.VTL.RH   Vertical block, right

Single vertical block to right side

94. B.VTR.LH   Vertical block, left

Single vertical block to left side

Suruchin Katas

This book includes all known katas for the suruchin; three traditional katas, and one created by the author (plus a basic exercise):

Tan (Short) Suruchin Kata – Originating from Ryukyu Kobudo (founded by Taira Shinken), this is the most common suruchin kata in the style. The kata is characterized by simple swinging techniques, done in repetitive sets. This kata shows the influence of the other weapons in Kobudo.

Naga (Long) Suruchin Kata – Also originating from Ryukyu Kobudo, this kata is nearly extinct; few in Ryukyu Kobudo practice the kata.

Suruchin no Toseki – This kata originates from Matayoshi Kobudo. It includes some of the more dramatic suruchin techniques, possibly showing an influence of the Shaolin meteor hammer (especially considering the founder of Matayoshi Kobudo learned the weapon in mainland China)

Miichiryu Suruchin Kata – This kata was created by the author to combine the more practical techniques of Ryukyu Kobudo, Matayoshi Kobudo, and Shaolin meteor hammer. The full description / history is included prior to the kata.

Suruchin Mini-Kata – This "kata" is a set of introductory techniques that can be used as an introduction to the suruchin for students. See description prior to kata for suggested applications of the kata.

Tan (Short) Suruchin Kata

Also called Mijikai Suruchin or Tan kusari no kata. This kata originates from Ryukyu Kobudo by way of Taira Shinken, and traditionally uses a metal (chain) suruchin with a handle on one end of approximately 150-152cm, or about 60 inches (not including the handle).

Figure 73 Taira Shinken with suruchin

Tan (Short) Suruchin Kata

1. Stand at attention; chain in gathered hold in left hand; handle reversed; bow H.LHG.RV

2. Left foot back; grab middle of loop with right hand, overhead block B.DBR.OH

3. Step up with left foot; double block right hand high. B.DBH.LS

Tan (Short) Suruchin Kata

4. Step up with right foot; double block left hand high. **B.DBH.RS**

5. Step up with left foot; double block right hand high. **B.DBH.LS**

6. Step up with right foot; figure 8 swing forward direction **S.FG8.FW**

Tan (Short) Suruchin Kata

7. Stall at lower right, reverse direction. Figure 8 reverse direction S.FG8.RV

8. Swing at right side, reverse direction S.RSD.RV

9. Stall in front; begin swinging in forward direction S.RSD.FW

Tan (Short) Suruchin Kata

10. Continue swinging and move to the left side, forward direction
S.LSD.FW

11. Stall at back; begin swinging in reverse direction at left side
S.LSD.RV

12. Transfer to swinging overhead, clockwise direction
S.OVH.CW

Tan (Short) Suruchin Kata

13. Allow to wrap around back to change directions

14. Swing overhead in counter-clockwise direction
S.OVH.CC

15. Right foot back & raise left foot; swing downward for leg check
B.LCH.LS

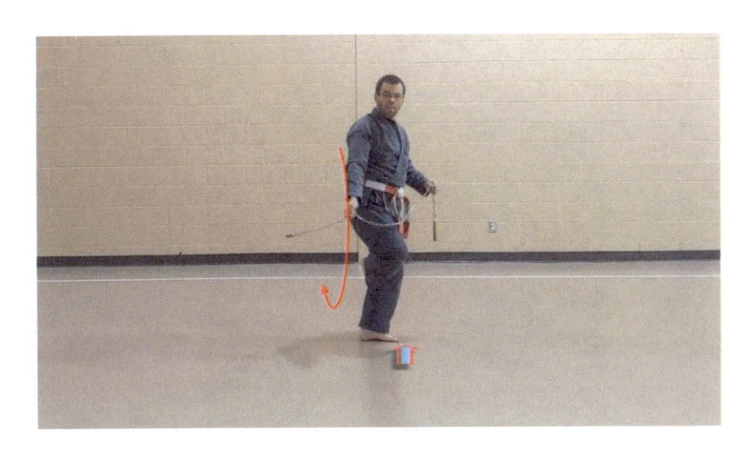

Tan (Short) Suruchin Kata

16. Step back with left foot & raise right foot; swing downward for leg check B.LCH.RS

17. Right foot back & raise left foot; swing downward for leg check B.LCH.LS

18. Step up with left foot then right foot; figure 8 swing forwards S.FG8.FW

Tan (Short) Suruchin Kata

19. Stall at right back; figure 8 swing in reverse direction S.FG8.RV

20. Continue swinging reverse direction at right side S.RSD.RV

21. Stall in front; start swinging forward direction S.RSD.FW

Tan (Short) Suruchin Kata

22. Continue to swing; move to left side, forward direction S.LSD.FW

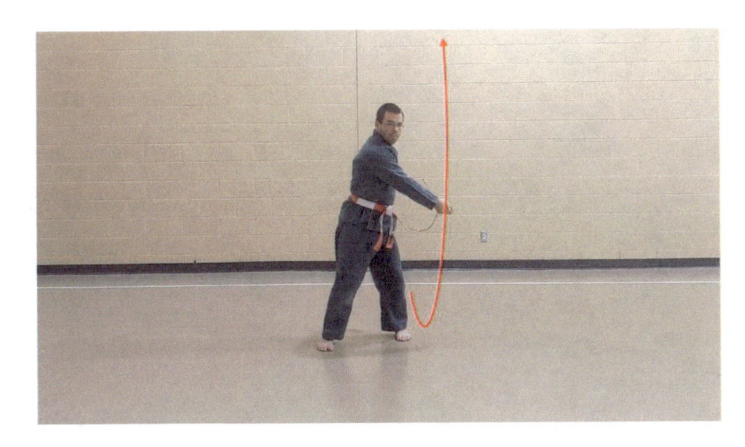

23. Stall at back; swing reverse direction S.LSD.RV

24. Transfer to overhead swing, clockwise direction S.OVH.CW

Tan (Short) Suruchin Kata

25. Allow to wrap around back to change directions

26. Overhead swing, counter-clockwise S.OVH.CC

27. Bring left hand to right hand to swing full-length counter clockwise S.EXT.CC

Tan (Short) Suruchin Kata

28. Pull left hand back to shorten swing
S.OVH.CC

29. Draw up with right foot; leg check to the right
B.LCH.RS

30. Continue swing into figure 8 pattern, forward direction
S.FG8.FW

Tan (Short) Suruchin Kata

31. Draw up with left foot; leg check to left side
B.LCH.LS

32. Set left foot down forwards; forward direction figure 8 swing with handle
S.HD8.FW

33. Step up with right foot; thrust with weight in right hand
C.WGT.1W

Tan (Short) Suruchin Kata

34. Left foot up as changing hands; thrust with weight in left hand
H.CHG. RH C.WGT.1W

35. Right foot up as changing hands; thrust with weight in right hand
H.CHG. LH C.WGT.1W

36. Step back with right foot; swing reverse direction at right side
S.RSD.RV

Tan (Short) Suruchin Kata

37. Upwards cast forward; shuffle forwards C.UPC.ST

38. Step backwards with left foot; swing reverse direction at left side S.LSD.RV

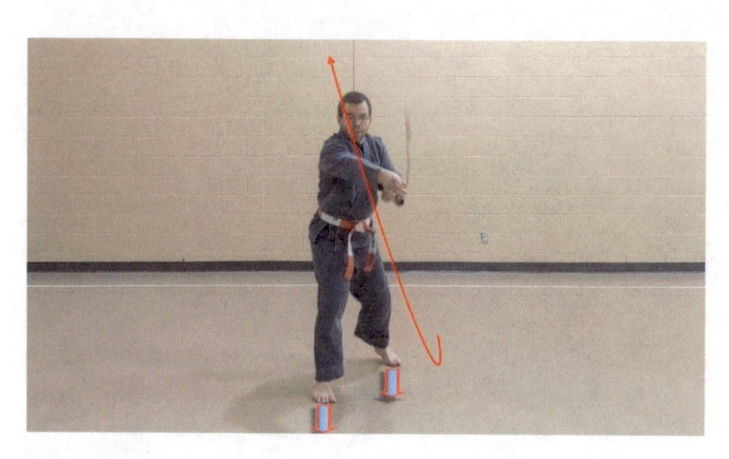

39. Upwards cast forwards; shuffle forward C.UPC.ST

Tan (Short) Suruchin Kata

40. Change handle direction to forwards; up with left foot, thrust with handle
H.SWH.FW
C.HDL.FW

41. Right foot up; figure 8 swing forwards; switch handle back
H.SWH.RV
S.FG8.FW

42. Catch weight in left hand, ending with doubled hold
S.CAT.LH

Tan (Short) Suruchin Kata

43. Step back with right foot; nunchuck style block to left side. B.NCH.LS

44. Step back with left foot; nunchuck style block to right side. B.NCH.RS

45. Shuffle forward; doubled high block B.DBR.OH

Tan (Short) Suruchin Kata

46. Gathered hold in right hand; stand at attention
H.GTH.RH

47. Bow. End of kata

Tan (Short) Suruchin Kata Summary

1. Gathered hold; bow H.LHG.RV	2. Left foot back B.DBR.OH	3. Left foot forward B.DBH.LS
4. Right foot forward B.DBH.RS	5. Left foot forward B.DBH.LS	6. Right foot forward S.FG8.FW
7. Stall; reverse swing S.FG8.RV	8. Swing right side S.RSD.RV	9. Stall; reverse swing S.RSD.FW
10. Left side swing S.LSD.FW	11. Stall; reverse swing S.LSD.RV	12. Overhead CW S.OVH.CW
13. Wrap around body to reverse	14. Overhead CCW S.OVH.CC	15. Right foot back B.LCH.LS

Tan (Short) Suruchin Kata Summary

16. Left foot back B.LCH.RS	17. Right foot back B.LCH.LS	18. Right foot forward S.FG8.FW
19. Stall; reverse swing S.FG8.RV	20. Right side swing S.RSD.RV	21. Stall; reverse swing S.RSD.FW
22. Switch to left side S.LSD.FW	23. Stall; reverse swing S.LSD.RV	24. Overhead CW S.OVH.CW
25. Wrap around body to reverse direction	26. Overhead CCW S.OVH.CC	27. Extended swing S.EXT.CC
28. Shorted swing S.OVH.CC	29. Right foot up B.LCH.RS	30. Figure 8 right S.FG8.FW

Tan (Short) Suruchin Kata Summary

31. Left foot up B.LCH.LS	32. Figure 8 with handle S.HD8.FW	33. Right foot forward C.WGT.1W
34. Left foot forward; switch grip C.WGT.1W	35. Right foot forward; switch grip C.WGT.1W	36. Right foot back S.RSD.RV
37. Shuffle forward C.UPC.ST	38. Left foot back S.LSD.RV	39. Shuffle forward C.UPC.ST
40. Left foot forward; switch grip C.HDL.FW	41. Right foot forward; switch grip S.FG8.FW	42. Catch in left hand S.CAT.LH
43. Right foot back B.NCH.LS	44. Left foot back B.NCH.RS	45. B.DBR.OH Bow out (not shown)

Naga (Long) Suruchin Kata

Alternative names are Cho Kusari no kata, Maezato no suruchin, or Kanegawa no Suruchin. This kata is from Ryukyu Kobudo and is the rarest suruchin kata to find performed today. It traditionally uses a metal (chain) suruchin with a handle on one end of approximately 230-240cm, or about 92-94 inches (not including the handle).

Note: In preparing this book for publication, influence from other weapon katas was noted in the author's performance of this kata; notably, holding the upper hand at shoulder height throughout vs. the traditional chin/ear height.

Figure 74 Motokatsu Inoue demonstrating bunkai, courtesy of Victor Smith.

Naga (Long) Suruchin Kata

1. Stand at attention, suruchin in left hand (gathered hold) H.LHG.RV

2. Bow

3. Pull left foot back, raise right foot; hold chain horizontally H.GTH.LH

Naga (Long) Suruchin Kata

4. Lower right foot forwards

5. Pivot both feet to the left; vertical block left hand high B.VTR.LH

6. Bring left foot up to right foot; right hand high

Naga (Long) Suruchin Kata

7. Step up with right foot; right hand forward

8. Step up with left foot; left hand forward

9. Step up with right foot; right hand forward

Naga (Long) Suruchin Kata

10. Pivot on right foot, moving left foot CCW; vertical block B.VTL.RH

11. Bring right foot next to left foot; vertical block B.VTR.LH

12. Slide right foot to the right

Naga (Long) Suruchin Kata

13. Bring left foot to right foot; vertical block B.VTL.RH

14. Step forward with right foot, right hand forward

15. Step forward with left foot, left hand forward

Naga (Long) Suruchin Kata

16. Step forward with right foot; right hand forward

17. Pivot on right foot, moving left foot CCW; vertical block B.VTL.RH

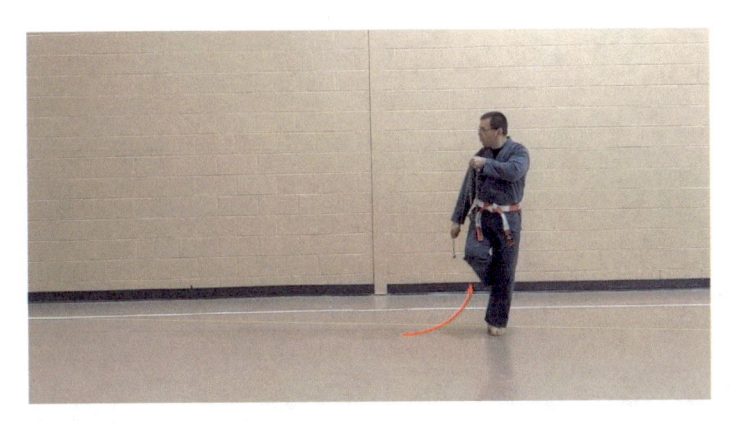

18. Draw right foot up; vertical block B.VTR.LH

Naga (Long) Suruchin Kata

19. Set right foot down; look left

20. Raise left foot; vertical block B.VTL.RH

21. Lower left foot parallel with right foot

Naga (Long) Suruchin Kata

22. Step up with right foot; right hand forward

23. Step up with left foot; left hand forward

24. Extend chain to midpoint; forward swing S.RSD.FW

Naga (Long) Suruchin Kata

25. Step forward with right foot; stop swinging

26. swing in overhead counter-clockwise circle S.OVH.CC

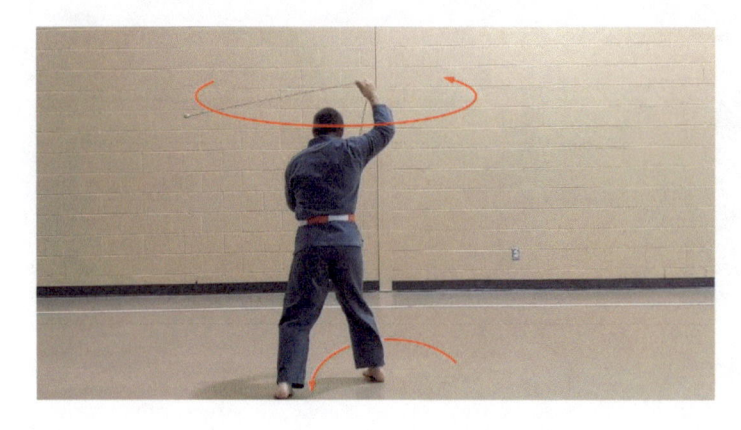

27. Continue swinging overhead; pivot on right foot to face back

Naga (Long) Suruchin Kata

28. Continue swinging; pivot on right foot forwards; extend chain S.EXT.CC

29. Shorten chain by pulling in with left hand

30. Stop swinging

Naga (Long) Suruchin Kata

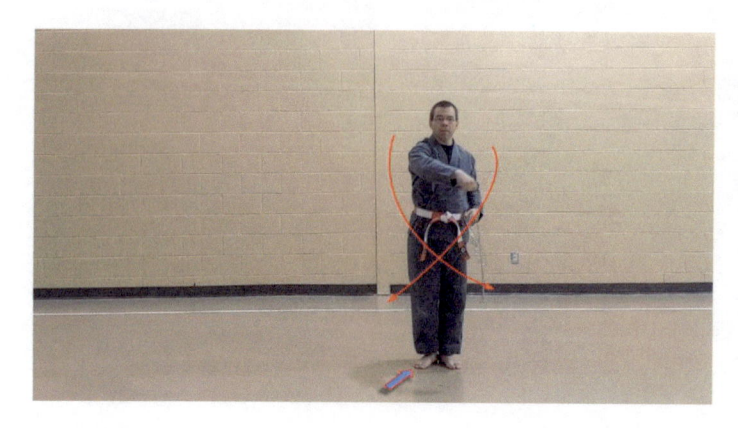

31. Draw right foot back to left foot; swing in forwards figure 8 pattern S.FG8.FW

32. Swing in forwards direction at right side S.RSD.FW

33. Swing at left side, forwards direction S.LSD.FW

Naga (Long) Suruchin Kata

34. Horizontal swing to right C.HZC.LS

35. Horizontal swing to left side C.HZC.RS

36. Step forwards with right foot; stop swinging

Naga (Long) Suruchin Kata

37. Bring right foot parallel to left foot; hold chain horizontally

38. Kneel on right knee; hold chain right hand up, left hand down

*Note: translation tells to "pull left foot back to kneel" – believed to be typo in original text

39. Stand back up; hold chain horizontally

154

Naga (Long) Suruchin Kata

40. Gather chain in right hand; attention stance
H.GTH.RH

41. Bow

42. End

Naga (Long) Suruchin Kata Summary

1. At attention H.LHG.RV	2. Bow	3. Left foot back, raise right H.GTH.LH
4. Right foot forwards	5. Pivot left; vertical block B.VTR.LH	6. Left foot up to right foot; right hand high
7. Right foot and hand forward	8. Left foot and hand forward	9. Right foot and hand forward
10. Pivot CCW on right foot B.VTL.RH	11. Right foot to left foot B.VTR.LH	12. Right foot to right
13. Left foot to right foot B.VTL.RH	14. Right foot and hand forward	15. Left foot and hand forward

Naga (Long) Suruchin Kata Summary

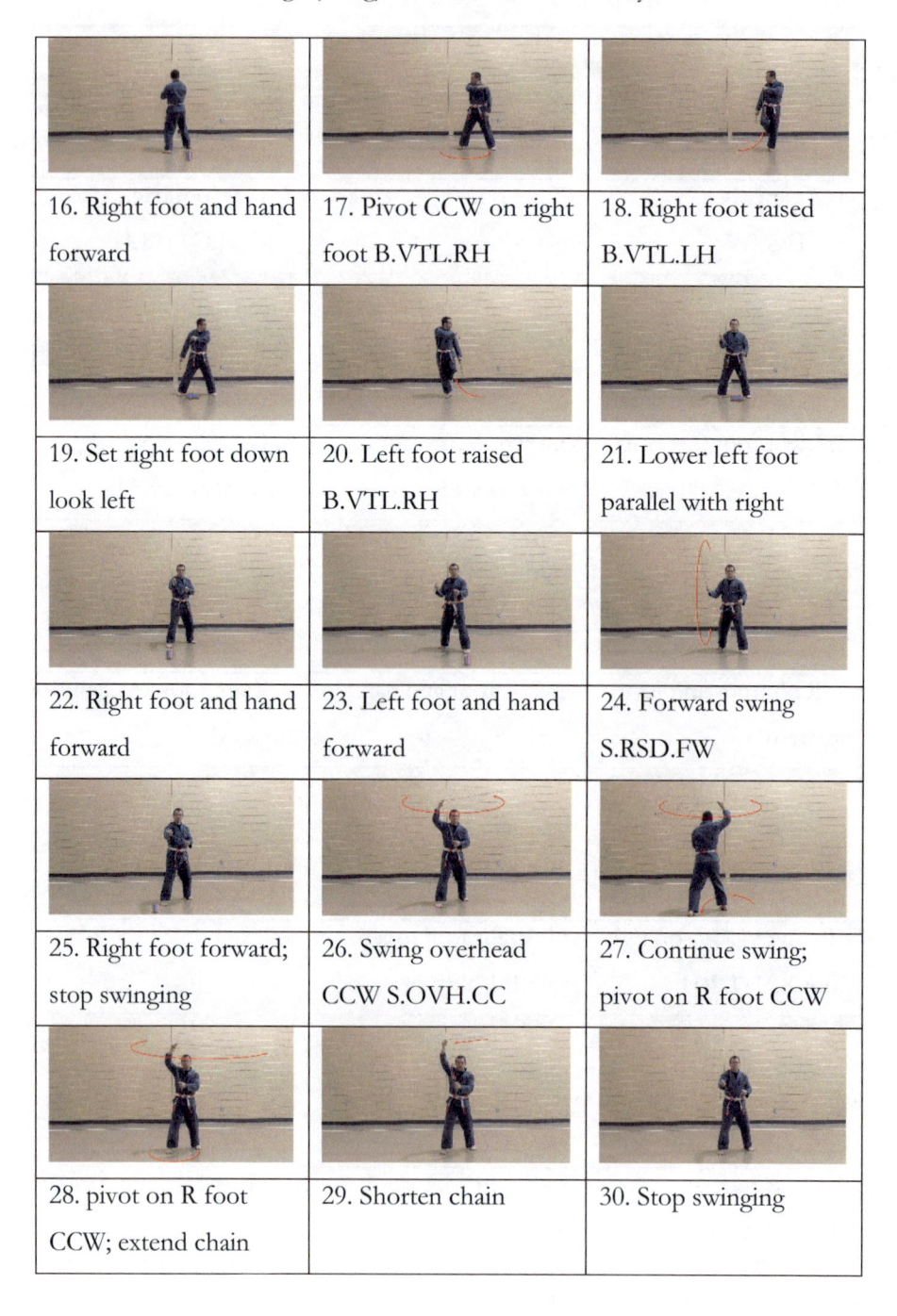

16. Right foot and hand forward	17. Pivot CCW on right foot B.VTL.RH	18. Right foot raised B.VTL.LH
19. Set right foot down look left	20. Left foot raised B.VTL.RH	21. Lower left foot parallel with right
22. Right foot and hand forward	23. Left foot and hand forward	24. Forward swing S.RSD.FW
25. Right foot forward; stop swinging	26. Swing overhead CCW S.OVH.CC	27. Continue swing; pivot on R foot CCW
28. pivot on R foot CCW; extend chain	29. Shorten chain	30. Stop swinging

Naga (Long) Suruchin Kata Summary

31. Right foot back S.FG8.FW	32. Forward swing S.RSD.FW	33. Left side forward swing S.LSD.FW
34. Horizontal swing to right C.HZC.LS	35. Horizontal swing to left side C.HZC.RS	36. Right foot forward; stop swinging
37. Right foot parallel with left	38. Kneel on right knee, chain vertical	39. Stand up, chain horizontal
40. At attention H.GTH.RH	41. Bow	42. End

Suruchin no Toseki

Also called Suruchin No Kata, this kata originates form Matayoshi Kobudo. It traditionally uses a rope and rock suruchin, measured to 1.5x the arm span of the practitioner (Image below of Matayoshi Shinpo courtesy of www.bushikan.com).

Note that some schools have developed variations of the kata (such as Sensei Andrea Guarelli's and Sensei Yamashiro Kenichi's versions); what follows is the version as documented in Matayoshi Shinpo's 1990's film [19].

Figure 75 Matayoshi Shinpo demonstrating suruchin technique, courtesy of www.bushikan.com

Suruchin No Toseki Kata

1. Stand at attention; suruchin gathered in thirds H.FLD.DB

2. Bow

3. Back to attention

Suruchin No Toseki Kata

4. Right foot forward; left hand up high block
B.DBH.RS

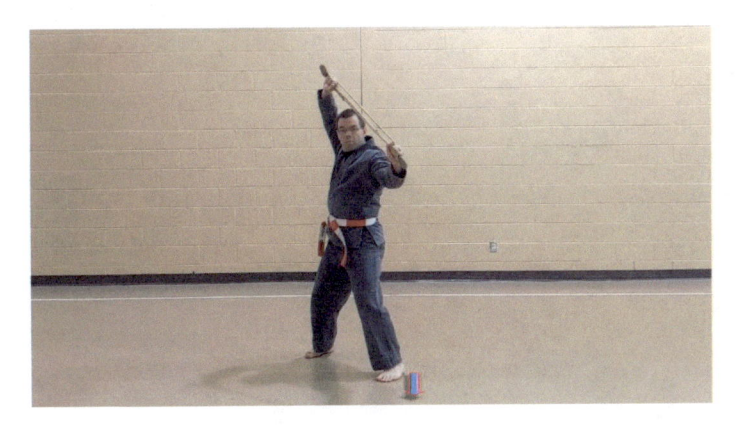

5. Left foot forward, right hand up high block
B.DBH.LS

6. Release with right hand, swing in left hand to cast forward horizontally
C.HZC.LS

Suruchin No Toseki Kata

7. Continue fully extended swing counter-clockwise S.EXT.CC

8. Shorten swing by drawing through right hand S.OVH.CC

9. Continue swing; pivot on left foot counter-clockwise to rear (180)

Suruchin No Toseki Kata

10. Continue pivot 90 degrees counter-clockwise

11. Continue pivot 90 degrees counter-clockwise to face front

12. Step up with right foot during forward horizontal cast….
C.HZC.LS

165

Suruchin No Toseki Kata

13. ... step up with left foot; forward cast again
C.HZC.LS

14. Stay stationary; forward cast a third time
C.HZC.LS

15. From overhead CCW swing, begin wrapping around right hand
H.WRP.RH

Suruchin No Toseki Kata

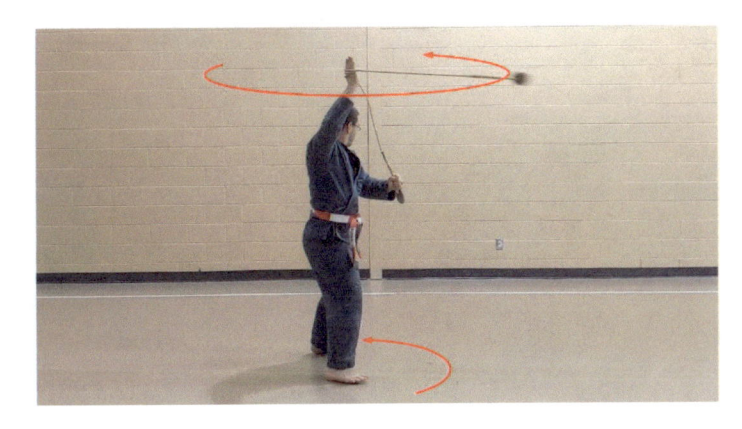

16. Continue wrapping, step back CCW with left foot

17. Continue wrapping, step 180 degrees CCW with right foot

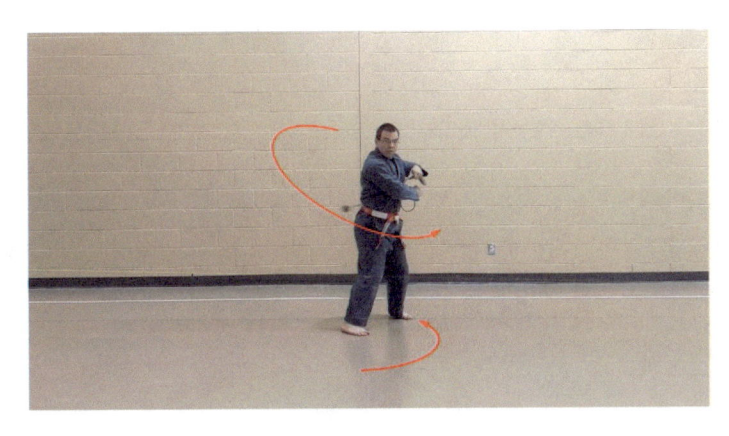

18. Finish wrapping, step back CCW with left foot, horizontal strike C.HZS.LS

Suruchin No Toseki Kata

19. Switch feet (up then back), swing CW overhead; horizontal strike C.HZS.RS

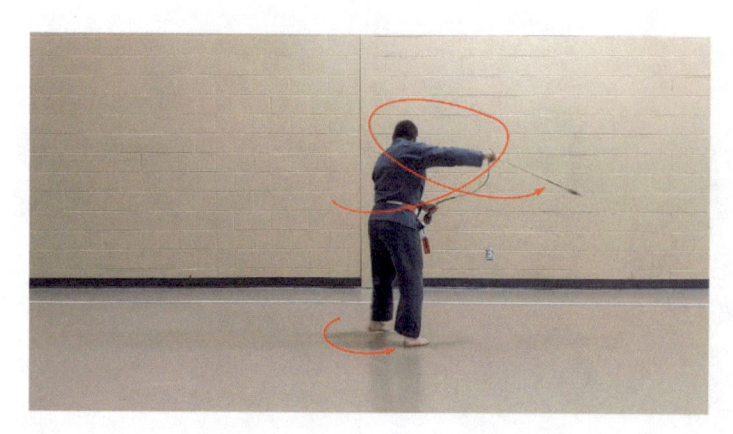

20. Step CCW with right foot, swing CCW overhead to prepare for…

21. …strike horizontally while drawing left foot back to kneel C.HZS.LS

Suruchin No Toseki Kata

22. Step up with left foot; swing overhead and strike horizontally C.HZS.RS

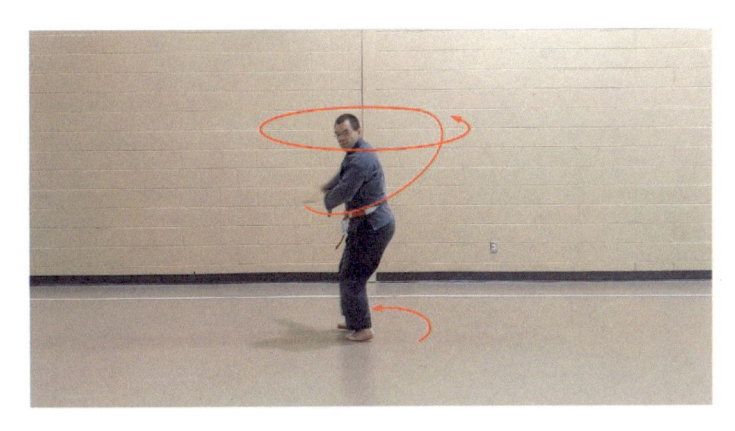

23. Swing CCW overhead as stepping CCW with right foot…

24. …step back with left foot, horizontal strike C.HZS.LS

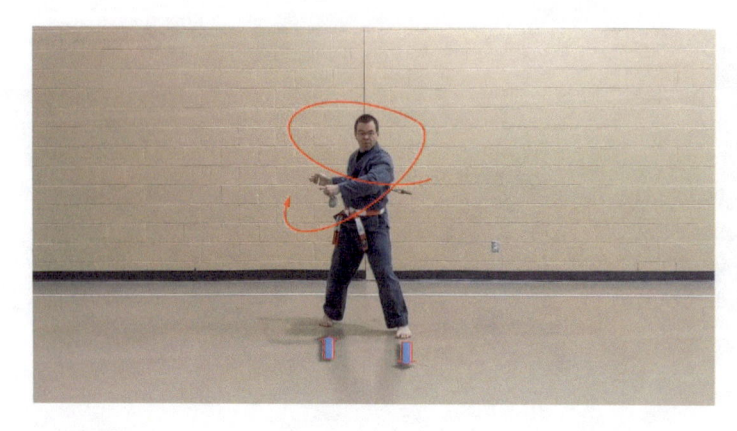

Suruchin No Toseki Kata

25. Switch feet (left up, right back); swing overhead & horizontal strike C.HZS.RS

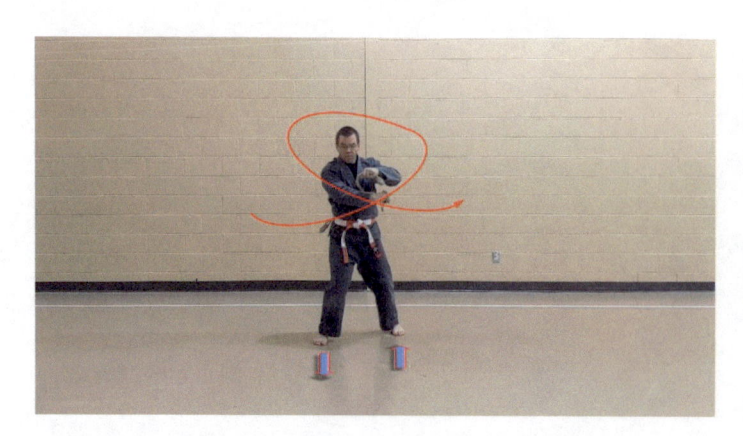

26. Switch feet (up then back); swing overhead & horizontal strike C.HZS.LS

27. Switch feet (left up, right back); swing overhead, horizontal strike C.HZS.RS

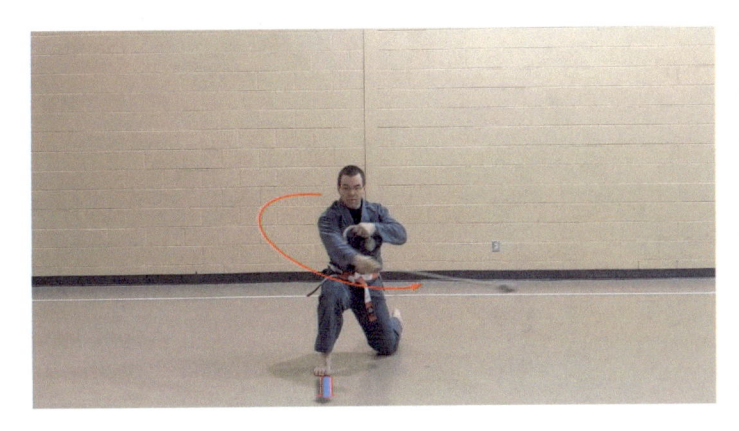

Suruchin No Toseki Kata

28. Step forward with right foot to kneeling, horizontal strike C.HZS.LS

29. Swing overhead and horizontal strike C.HZS.RS

30. Horizontal strike to left side C.HZS.LS

Suruchin No Toseki Kata

31. Stand up; swing overhead and horizontal strike C.HZS.RS

32. Swing overhead and horizontal strike C.HZS.LS

33. Swing overhead clockwise to unwind suruchin from hand

Suruchin No Toseki Kata

34. Swing forward direction at right side 2x
S.RSD.FW

35. Swing forward direction at left side 1x
S.LSD.FW

36. Swing forward direction at right side 2x
S.RSD.FW

Suruchin No Toseki Kata

37. Swing forward direction at left side 1x S.LSD.FW

38. Swing forward direction at right side 2x S.RSD.FW

39. Extend rope in left hand, double forwards swing S.DBL.FW

Suruchin No Toseki Kata

40. Step back with left foot; double weight swing to left C.DBL.LS

41. Switch feet (up then back); circle overhead and double strike to right C.DBL.RS

Note: overhead rotation path of both weights not shown with arrows for clarity's sake; same through step #48

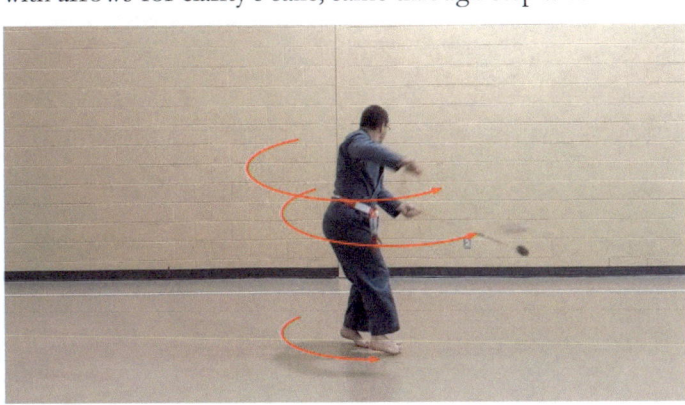

42. Step CCW with right foot while swinging weights CCW…

175

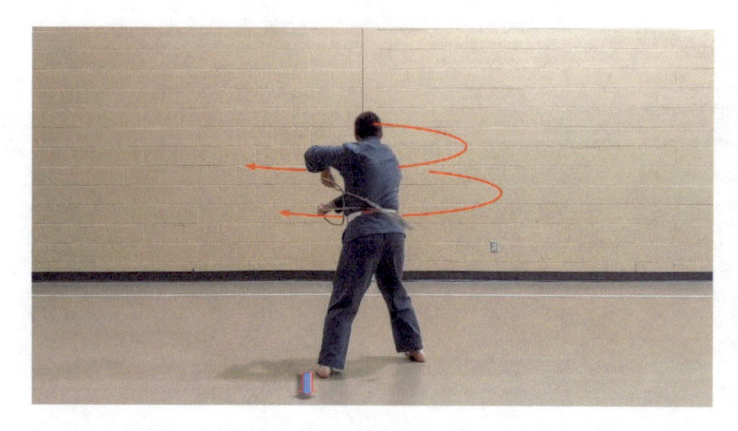

Suruchin No Toseki Kata

43. …circle both weights overhead and side strike; left foot back C.DBL.LS

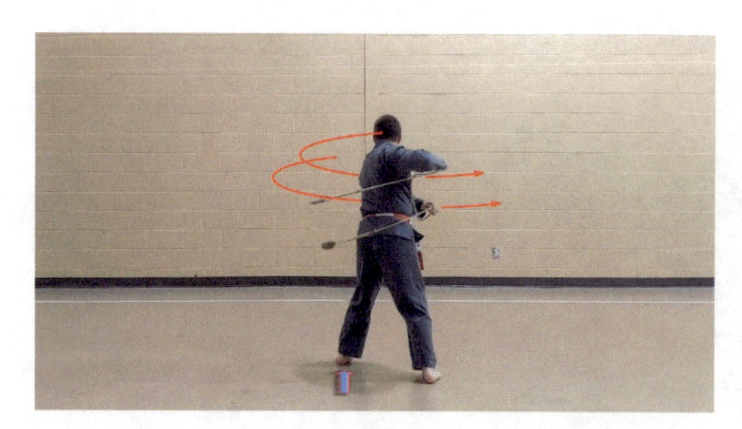

44. Step up with left foot, circle both weight overhead and side strike C.DBL.RS

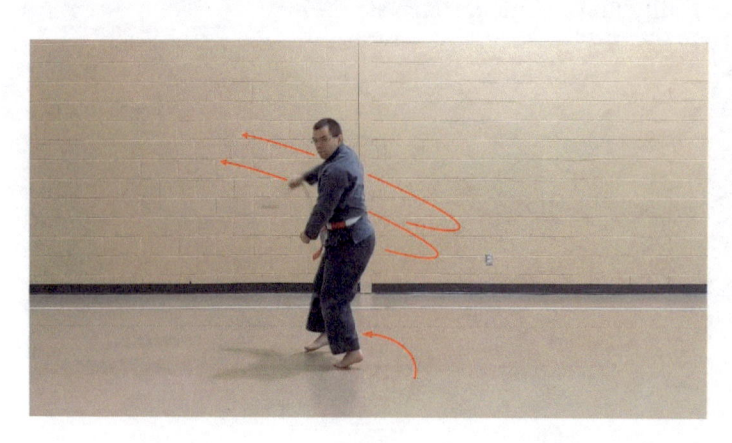

45. Step CCW with right foot, start swinging weights CCW…

Suruchin No Toseki Kata

46. ... step back with left foot; circle weights overhead and side strike C.DBL.LS

47. Switch feet (left up, right back), circle weights overhead and side strike C.DBL.RS

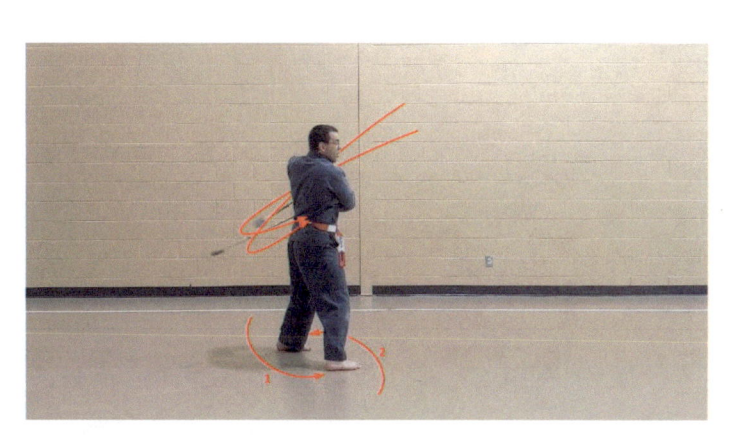

48. Step CCW with right then left foot to face side, circle overhead & side strike C.DBL.LS

Suruchin No Toseki Kata

49. Turn CW (left then right foot); adjust to standard hold, forward swing S.RSD.FW

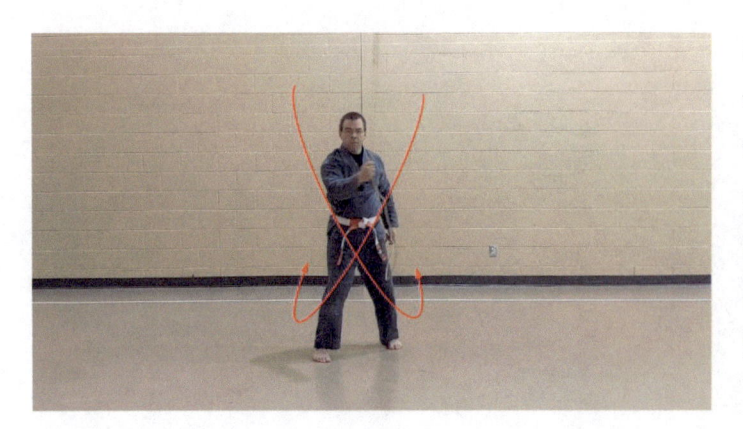

50. Step up with right foot; figure 8 swing in forwards direction S.FG8.FW

51. Double figure 8 S.DBL.F8

Suruchin No Toseki Kata

52. Spin CCW while transitioning to standard hold; overhead CCW swing S.OVH.CC

53. Continue turn to face forward; continue overhead CCW swing S.OVH.CC

54. Shuffle forward and horizontal cast right to left C.HZC.LS

Suruchin No Toseki Kata

55. Open right hand to wrap suruchin
H.WRP.RH

56. Catch swinging weight with left hand
S.CAT.LH
Step up with right foot and…

57. Strike with right hand

Suruchin No Toseki Kata

58. Bring left foot up parallel with right foot

59. Bring left foot next to right, attention stance; suruchin in right hand

60. Bow (end)

Suruchin No Toseki Kata Summary

1. Attention H.FLD.DB	2. Bow	3. Attention
4. Right foot forward B.DBH.RS	5. Left foot forward B.DBH.LS	6. Release right hand C.HZC.RS
7. Overhead CCW swing S.EXT.CC	8. Overhead swing S.OVH.CC	9. Pivot CCW on left foot 180 degrees
10. Pivot CCW on left foot 90 degrees	11. Pivot CCW on left foot 90 degrees to front	12. Right foot forward C.HZC.LS
13. Left foot forward C.HZC.LS	14. Forward cast C.HZC.LS	15. Wrap around hand H.WDB.RH

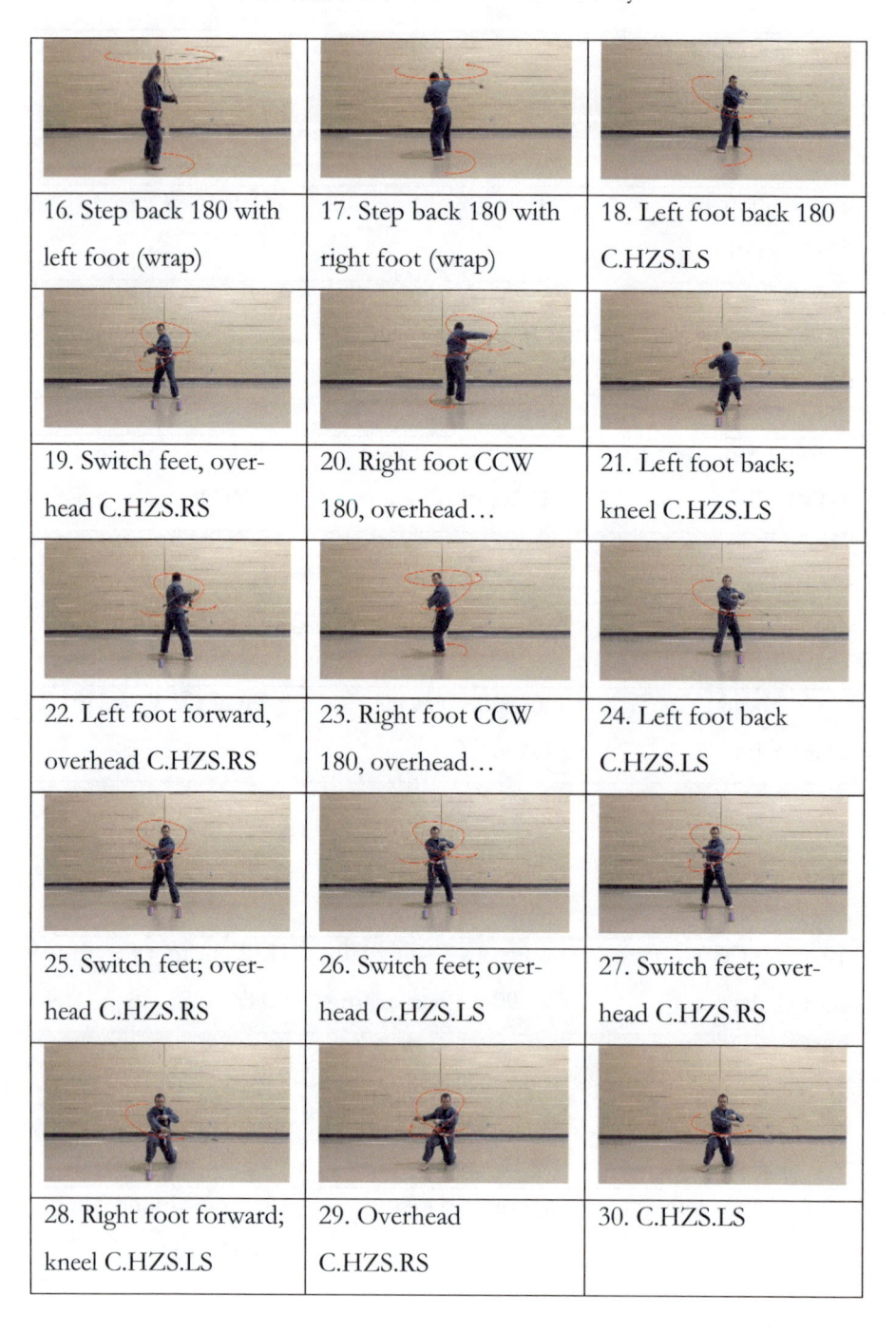

Suruchin No Toseki Kata Summary

16. Step back 180 with left foot (wrap)	17. Step back 180 with right foot (wrap)	18. Left foot back 180 C.HZS.LS
19. Switch feet, overhead C.HZS.RS	20. Right foot CCW 180, overhead…	21. Left foot back; kneel C.HZS.LS
22. Left foot forward, overhead C.HZS.RS	23. Right foot CCW 180, overhead…	24. Left foot back C.HZS.LS
25. Switch feet; overhead C.HZS.RS	26. Switch feet; overhead C.HZS.LS	27. Switch feet; overhead C.HZS.RS
28. Right foot forward; kneel C.HZS.LS	29. Overhead C.HZS.RS	30. C.HZS.LS

Suruchin No Toseki Kata Summary

31. Stand, overhead C.HZS.RS	32. Overhead C.HZS.LS	33. CW swing to unwrap
34. Forward swing 2x S.RSD.FW	35. Left side swing 1x S.LSD.FW	36. Forward swing 2x S.RSD.FW
37. Left side swing 1x S.LSD.FW	38. Forward swing 2x S.RSD.FW	39. Double forward swing S.DBL.FW
40. Left foot back C.DBL.LS	41. Switch feet; overhead C.DBL.RS	42. Right foot CCW 180; overhead…
43. Left foot back C.DBL.LS	44. Left foot forward, overhead C.DBL.RS	45. Right foot CCW 180; overhead…

Suruchin No Toseki Kata Summary

46. Left foot back C.DBL.LS	47. Switch feet, overhead C.DBL.RS	48. Turn 90 CCW; overhead C.DBL.LS
49. Turn 90 CW S.RSD.FW	50. Right foot forward S.FG8.FW	51. Double figure 8 S.DBL.F8
52. Spin 180 CCW…	53. turn 180 CCW S.OVH.CC	54. Shuffle forward C.HZC.LS
55. Wrap suruchin H.WRP.RH	56. Catch in left hand S.CAT.LH	57. Right foot forward, strike right hand
58. Left foot forward	59. Left foot to right foot; rope in right hand	60. Bow (end)

Miichiryu Suruchin Kata

Introduction to Miichiryu Suruchin kata

In the world of martial arts, it is rare to get an insight into the mind of the creator of a kata, to know the exact thought process that went into the kata's creation. It is with that in mind that the author includes the following description of Miichiryu (mee-chee-roo) kata:

Authors Note:

This kata was designed to combine the movements of Ryukyu Kobudo, Matayoshi Kobudo, and Meteor Hammer. This is reflected in the name, which translates to "Three Styles suruchin." No single style included the full range of potent suruchin techniques. As far as the footwork, this kata uses the Naihunchin kata pattern. This was done for three reasons; first, the pattern works well with several of the techniques (leg check, foot casting, etc.). Second, this pattern does not roam around much. Considering how much room is needed to swing a suruchin, conserving space was a priority for practicality in the dojo. Third, the pattern is already known to the students of my dojo, being Isshinryu, making one less thing to learn. As far as techniques go, while there are some fantastic and powerful techniques available, I restricted some categories for practicality's sake. I tried to avoid movements that overly wrapped around the body, since an attacker rushing forward and interrupting a movement would leave you at a severe disadvantage. I also avoided techniques that took several seconds to prepare (wrapping/spinning getting ready for a cast) for the same reason. Lastly, there are two forms of casting with the foot; letting the weight rest on the lower half of the foot and then casting the weight with a kick or hitting higher up the rope and letting the weight make a tight circle past the foot to cast. While the second method generates significant centrifugal force, the first method is less susceptible to failing if positioning is not perfect and allows casting in directions other than the initial swing direction. Lastly, this kata is not intended to be the last word in all the best techniques for suruchin, but a starting place that a student can then add additional katas and techniques to as they progress.

Regards,

    Leo Scott Britt III

Miichiryu Kata

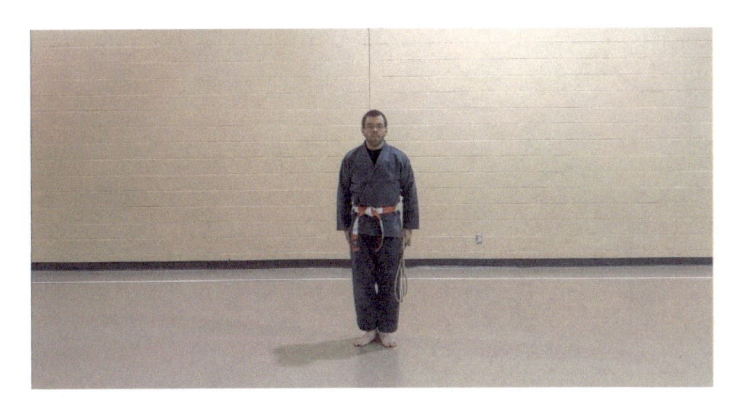

1. Stand at attention; suruchin in gathered hold in left hand handle reversed H.LHG.RV

2. Bow

3. Salutation (right hand flat over left hand)

Miichiryu Kata

4. Look to left; feet come together

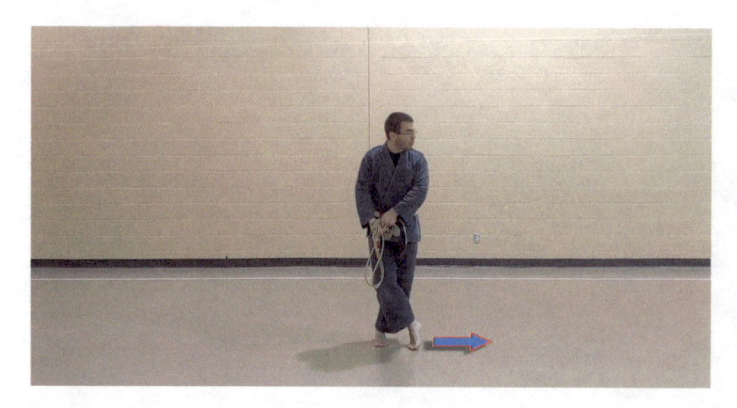

5. Step across with right foot, while grabbing middle of rope with right hand

6. Step out to left with left foot, block to left side B.DBL.LS

Miichiryu Kata

7. Release weight with left hand; swing at side in forward direction S.RSD.FW

8. Continue swinging and step across to the right with left foot

9. Bring right foot up (toes out) and catch suruchin 3-4" up rope

Miichiryu Kata

10. Kick out with right foot to cast weight forward at head height
C.FOT.FW

11. Return to forward swing at side, look back over right shoulder
S.RSD.FW

12. Upward cast to the back
C.UPC.BK

Miichiryu Kata

13. Return to side spin, this time in the reverse direction
S.RSD.RV

14. Upward cast in the forward direction at head height
C.UPC.ST

15. Resume spinning at side, forward direction
S.RSD.FW

Miichiryu Kata

16. Extend right foot, toes out and catch suruchin 3-4" up rope

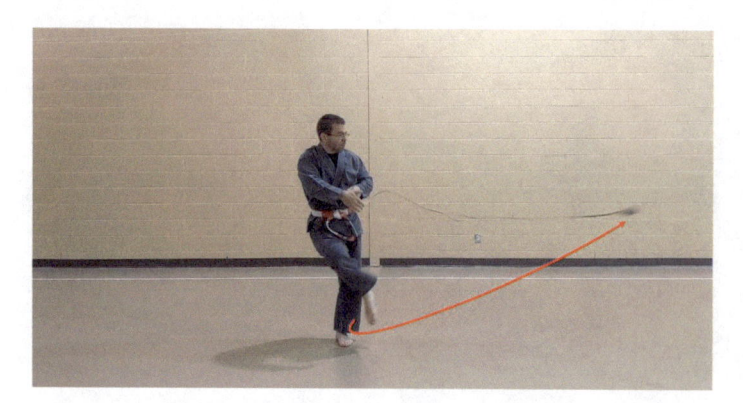

17. Kick right foot to the left to cast weight to left C.FOT.LS

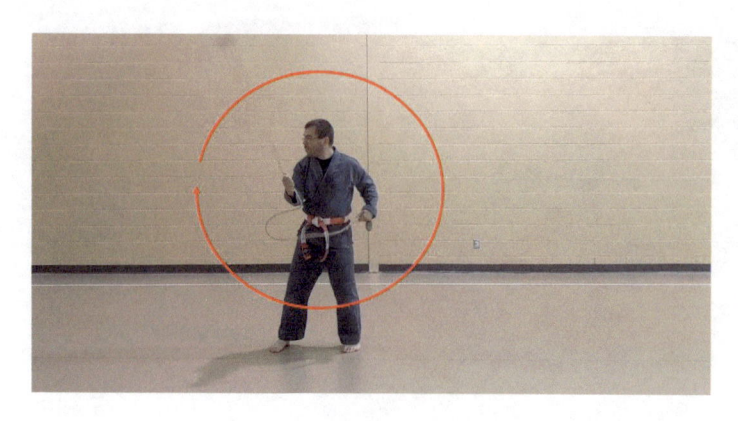

18. Recover rope and swing in a circle in front, CCW S.FRT.CC

Miichiryu Kata

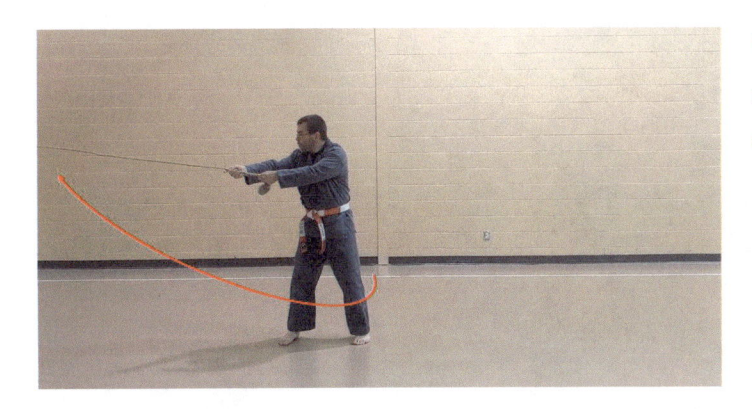

19. Cast to right side
C.UPC.RS

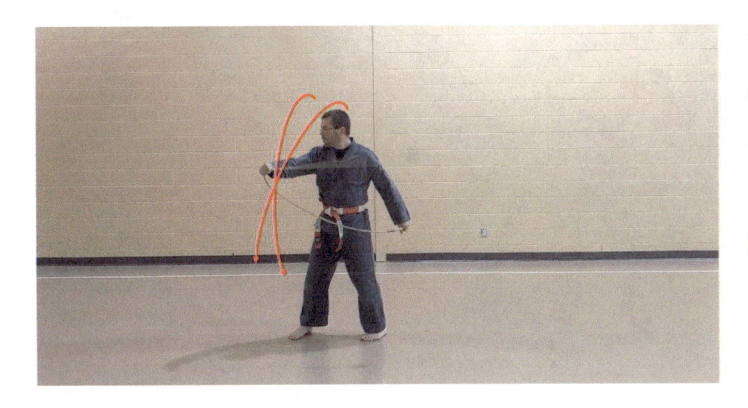

20. Pivot 45 degrees; swing in figure 8 pattern forwards direction
S.FG8.FW

21. Swing at right side in forwards direction; look left
S.RSD.FW

Miichiryu Kata

22. Extend right elbow into path of rope so suruchin swings up into it

23. Pivot feet to other 45; at same time move elbow to front of body S.ELB.FW

24. Look right, extend elbow into path of rope so it comes down on it

Miichiryu Kata

25. As weight comes up, lean back slightly, and move elbow out while…

26. …Pivoting feet to other 45, continue forward swing S.ELB.RV

27. Pivot feet to front and swing overhead clockwise S.OVH.CW

Miichiryu Kata

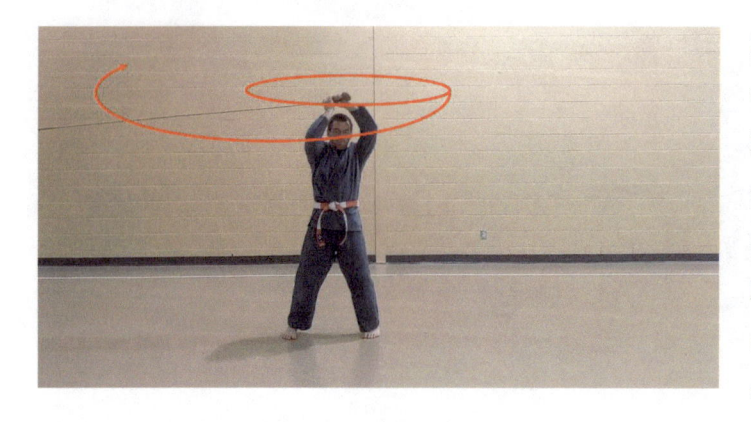

28. Bring the left hand to the right hand for a full-length overhead swing S.EXT.CW

29. Release with left hand; continue swing lower…

30. …Continue swing around back, reach to catch with left hand

Miichiryu Kata

31. Transfer to left hand, bring right hand to front to catch rope
S.BCK.CW

32. Continue movement into overhead clockwise swing
S.OVH.CW

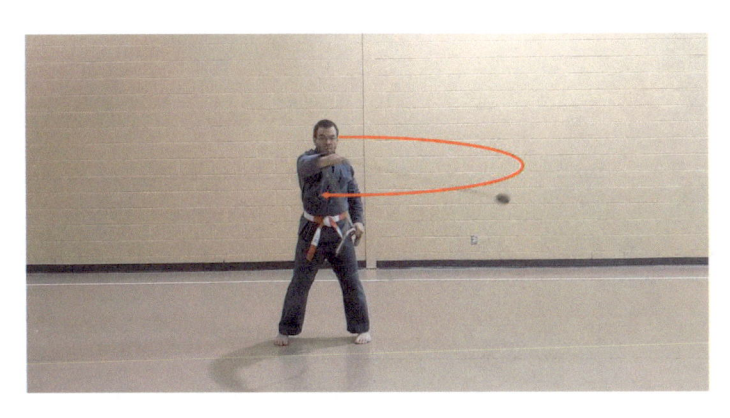

33. Swinging strike to front, left to right
C.HZS.RS

Miichiryu Kata

34. Allow weight to wrap body and be stopped by arm to change directions

35. Swing back around and over-head, counter-clockwise S.OVH.CC

36. Look to the left

Miichiryu Kata

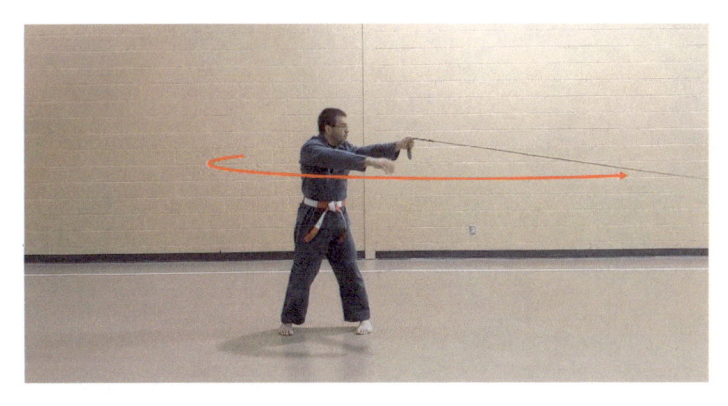

37. Cast to the left with right-to-left horizontal swing
C.HZC.LS

38. Shorten up rope; continue swinging overhead; look right
S.OVH.CC

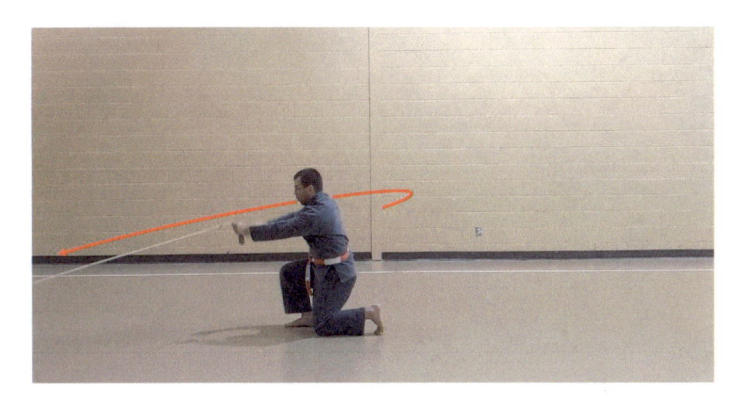

39. Kneel on left knee; cast to right (right-to-left swing)
C.HCZ.LS

Miichiryu Kata

40. Stand back up; continue swing overhead counter-clockwise S.OVH.CC

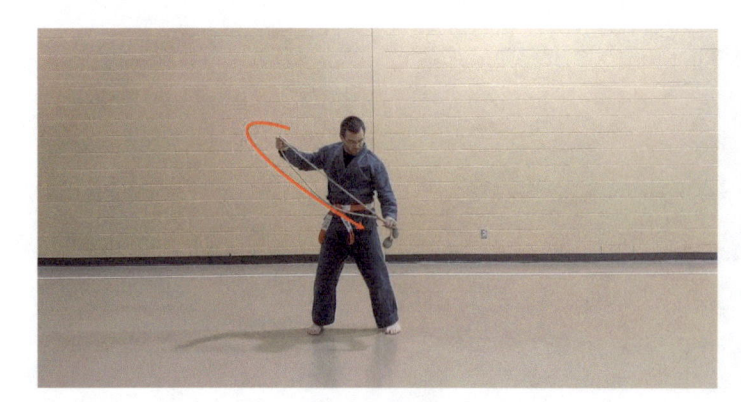

41. Swing weight down to meet left hand, catch S.CAT.LH

42. Doubled high block to the right; left hand high B.DBL.RS

Miichiryu Kata

43. Stack both hands on the right hip; look left

44. Release weight to allow it to hang down about 1 foot

45. Step across to the left with the right foot

Miichiryu Kata

46. Bring left foot up; swing weight down in block **B.LCH.LS**

47. Set left foot down; doubled rope high block **B.DBR.OH**

48. Catch right pinky finger in loop; look left

Miichiryu Kata

49. Wrap doubled rope around right hand one time
H.WDB.RH

50. High block to the left, right hand high
B.DBL.LS (modified)

51. Release weights with left hand; swing clockwise to left side
C.DBS.LS (modified)

Miichiryu Kata

52. Allow weights to wrap around body to change directions

53. Swing weights back in clockwise direction over head

54. Swing left to right; wrap around body C.DBS.RS (modified)

Miichiryu Kata

55. Swing back overhead, & strike right - left; weights wrap C.DBS.LS (modified)

56. Left hand regains control of weights

57. Double high block; rope still wrapped around right hand B.DBR.OH (modified)

Miichiryu Kata

58. Loop rope forward in catching movement

59. Wrap rope around right elbow, look left B.NCH.RS

60. Sweep up with left foot

Miichiryu Kata

61. Set left foot down; strike to left with weights in left hand. **Kiai (yell)** C.WGT.DB

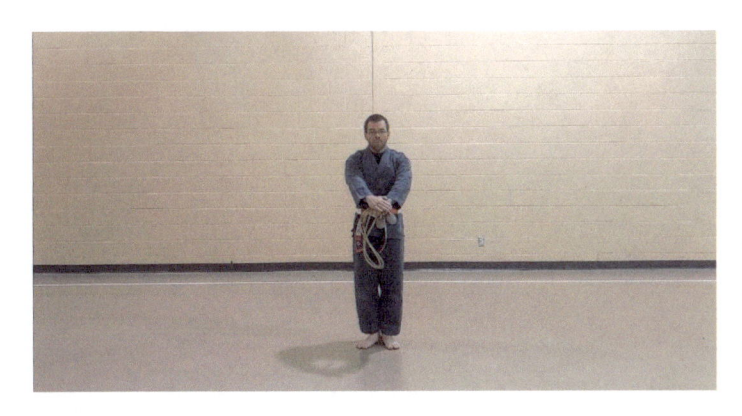

62. Bring feet together, release wrapped rope and gather, right hand open over left

63. Bow. End of kata

Miichiryu Summary

2. Bow H.LHG.RV	3. Salutation	4. Look left; feet together
5. Right foot step across	6. Left foot step out B.DBH.RS	7. Look right; spin forward S.RSD.FW
8. Left foot step across	9. Catch rope on right foot	10. Cast forward C.FOT.FW
11. Look over right shoulder S.RSD.FW	12. Cast backwards C.UPC.BK	13. Spin in reverse direction S.RSD.RV
14. Upward cast, forward C.UPC.ST	15. Spin forwards S.RSD.FW	16. Catch rope on right foot; look left

Miichiryu Summary

17. Kicking cast to left C.FOT.LS	18. Circle in front, clockwise S.FRT.CW	19. Upward cast to right C.UPC.RS
20. Fig. 8 swing, right 45 S.FG8.FW	21. Look left; forward swing S.RSD.FW	22. Extend right elbow to catch rope
23. Pivot to left 45 S.ELB.FW	24. Look right; extend right elbow	25. Lean back; move elbow around…
26. Pivot to right 45 S.ELB.RV	27. Feet to front; swing overhead S.OVH.CW	28. Extended overhead swing S.EXT.CW
29. Release with left hand	30. Swing behind back; switch to left hand	31. Swing to front; catch rope right hand

Miichiryu Summary

32. Overhead clockwise swing S.OVH.CW	33. Left to right strike C.HZS.RS	34. Weight wrap around body
35. Overhead counter-clockwise S.OVH.CC	36. Look left	37. Right to left strike C.HZC.LS
38. Overhead counter-clockwise S.OVH.CC	39. Kneeling right to left strike C.KNE.RS	40. Overhead counter-clockwise S.OVH.CC
41. Catch weight in left hand H.LHG.RV	42. Double block to right B.DBH.LS	43. Stack hand on right hip, look right
44. Lower weight 1 foot	45. Step across with right foot	46. Leg block (left foot up) B.LCH.LS

Miichiryu Summary

47. Doubled high block B.DBR.OH	48. Catch right pinky in loop, look left	49. Wrap once around right hand H.WDB.RH
50. High block left B.DBH.RH	51. Release left hand; swing left C.DBS.LS	52. Wrap around body
53. Swing clockwise overhead	54. Swing left to right; wrap C.DBS.RS	55. Swing right to left; wrap C.DBS.LS
56. Left hand grab weights	57. Overhead block B.DBR.OH	58. Looping forward
59. Wrap around right elbow B.NCH.RS	60. Sweep up left foot	61. Strike with weights Bow out (not shown)

Suruchin Mini-Kata

About Mini Katas

The concept of mini katas came about from students who joined karate with the hopes of working on a particular weapon they had dreamed of learning. However, in the author's Isshinryu school a student does not traditionally start on weapons until at least green belt. This could be discouraging for some students. However, the rank requirements already included an "extra credit" requirement for many ranks that could be fulfilled by attending a seminar, attending a tournament, writing a paper, etc. So "mini-katas" were created for all weapons as an option for extra credit. These katas were designed to be 12 moves or less, could be learned in a single class, and would serve as an introduction to the weapon with some of the basic blocks and strikes for that weapon. This gives students an option to learn about what interests them at an earlier stage and whets the appetite for the full katas that come further down the road.

While the dynamics of the suruchin make it a more difficult weapon to master than, say, the Bo, it is by no means beyond the reach of students who wish to apply themselves. To prove this point, the photos in this kata are of Ian, a six-year-old student who took an interest in the suruchin and took it upon himself to learn it and become proficient at it (in addition to his normal curriculum).

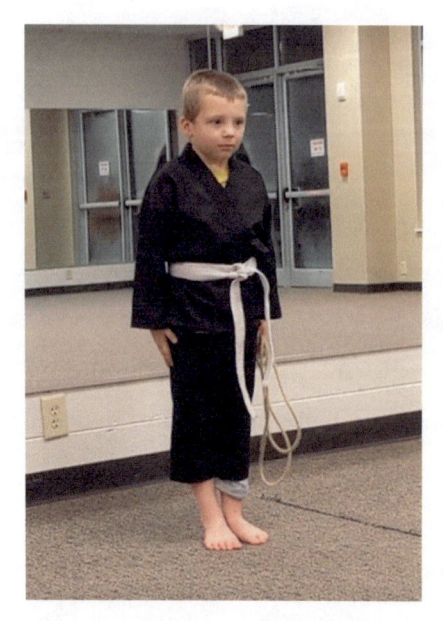

Suruchin Mini-Kata

1. Bow in

2. Step back with left foot; overhead block

3. Swing in forward figure of 8 (2x)

4. Reverse direction, reverse swing at side 2x

Suruchin Mini-Kata

5. Cast forward

6. Swing counterclockwise overhead 2x

7. Cast forward

8. Swing forward at side 2x

217

Suruchin Mini-Kata

9. Cast forward with right foot

10. Resume swinging forward at side

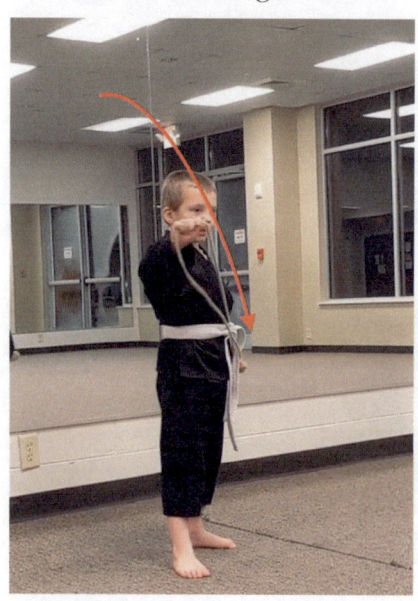

11. Catch weight with left hand

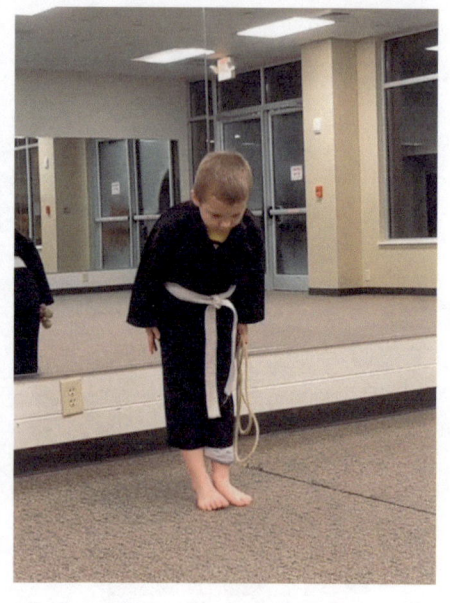

12. Bow out

Kumite

The following section demonstrates example applications (Bunkai) for the suruchin techniques, inclusive of various styles and suruchin types. It is in no way intended to be comprehensive of all the ways to use a suruchin.

#	Technique Name	Page
1	Forward figure 8 against bo, to outside	208
2	Forward figure 8 against bo, to inside	209
3	Double block to outside against bo	210
4	Double block to inside against bo	211
5	Single block to inside against bo	212
6	Single block to outside against bo	213
7	Single leg block against bo	214
8	Double neck wrap to throw	215
9	Trap weapon, switch and strike	216
10	Entangle leg and throw	217

Technique 1: Forward figure 8 against bo, to outside

1. Figure 8 swing; strike head/collar bone as suruchin is at right side

2. Opponent raises bo to try to guard

3. Step up; strike with weight to midsection

Technique 2: Forward figure 8 against bo, to inside

1. Figure 8 swing; strike head/collar bone as suruchin is at right side

2. Opponent raises bo to try to guard

3. Step up and to side; strike with weight to kidney area

Technique 3: Double block to outside against bo

1. Double block (parry) bo to right

2. Release one weight and swing forwards to head/ collar bone

3. Step to side; strike to kidney area

Technique 4: Double block to inside against bo

1. Double block bo to left side

2. Release one weight and swing forwards strike head/collar bone

3. Step up; strike with other weight to midsection

Technique 5: Single block to inside against bo

1. Single bock (parry) bo to left side

2. Swing free end down on head/ collar bone

3. Step up; strike with other weight to midsection

Technique 6: Single block to outside against bo

1. Single block bo (parry) to right side

2. Swing free end down on head/ collar bone

3. Step to side; strike with other weight to kidney area

Technique 7: Single leg block against bo

1. Hold rope 8-12" from end in right hand

2. Parry bo with right leg raised

3. Step forward and strike with weight in right hand

Technique 8: Double neck wrap to throw

1. Holding suruchin in 3rds (manriki length), head block

2. Force forwards; trapping hand as wrap around back of neck

3. Pivot body (hip-to-hip); throw opponent

Technique 9: Trap weapon, switch and strike

1. Swing and wrap weapon

2. Maintain tension, step forward and grab rope with left hand (let go of left weight)

3. Step forward and strike with weight using right hand

Technique 10: Entangle leg and throw

1. Horizontal swing to wrap lead leg

2. Pull to take down opponent

3. Step forward; strike with other weight to head

Training Methods

Below are a few ideas for training with the suruchin, both solo and in the dojo. For most methods of practice other than solo kata, some form of practice suruchin is suggested. See the "Construction" section of this book for ideas on making a practice suruchin.

1. **Kobudo Dummy**. A relatively inexpensive Kobudo dummy can by formed using 2x4 lumber made into a cross shape with a short crosspiece, which is then wrapped in rope. This is good for both light and full contact practice (once the student is capable enough to use a heavy suruchin without hurting themselves). The dummy below was made with 2x4 and 2x10 lumber and wrapped in carpet, and includes a hole at head height for target practice with casting techniques.

Figure 76 Kobudo Dummy

2. **Floor targets.** These inexpensive rubber/poly discs (sometimes called Spot Markers or Carpet Spots) can provide safe targets for younger/more inexperienced students, especially with the tennis ball type suruchin.

Figure 77 Spot markers

3. **"Ladder ball" PVC pipe.** This configuration of ¾" PVC pipe which is similar to the game Ladder Ball can be used by two students at once to cast and wrap around various parts, or to cast through various openings for target practice.

Figure 78 PVC Target

4. **Begleri.** This traditional Greek skill toy provides an excellent compact and portable way for beginners to gain an intuitive sense of the physics involved in a weighted rope. This training aid can be easily aquired. A brief history from www.aroundsquare.com:

> "Begleri (Greek: μπεγλέρι) originated in Greece, as an adaptation of traditional Greek worry beads, or "komboloi". Like other rosary-style worry beads, komboloi consist of a string of beads joined into a closed loop, often with a larger ornamental bead or tassels at the end. In Greece, there is a long tradition of flipping the komboloi around and between the fingers, to pass the time and keep the hands busy and the mind at ease. Skilled komboloi players are able to perform tricks and patterns as the beads pass rhythmically between the fingers."

Figure 79 Begleri, used with permission from www.aroundsquare.com

233

Resources

[1] Alexander, George (director), Motokatsu Inoue (performer) (2007). *Ryukyu Kobujutsu*. DVD.

[2] Bishop, Mark (2017). *Okinawan Weaponry: Hidden Methods, Ancient Myths of Kobudo & Te*. ISBN-13 : 978-1326916749

[3] Clarke, Christopher M. (2013). *Okinawan Kobudo: A history of weaponry styles and masters*. Clarke's Canyon Press, Huntingtown MD. ISBN-13: 978-1480264366

[4] Draeger, Donn F. (1972). *The Weapons and Fighting Arts of Indonesia*. Tuttle Martial Arts. ISBN-13 : 0-8048-1716-2.

[5] Guarelli, Andrea (2016). *Okinawan Kobudo: The History, Tools and Techniques of the Ancient Martial Art*. Skyhorse. ISBN-13 : 978-1634504843

[6] Heinze, Thomas (2009). *The Meister des Karate und Kobudo. Teil 1: before 1900*. Norderstedt, Germany: Books on Demand GmbH. EAN 9783839117859

[7] Lohse, Frederick W. (2014). *The Matayoshi Family and Kingai-ryu*. Meibukan Magazine. https://kodokanboston.files.wordpress.com/2014/02/kingairyuarticle.pdf

[8] Lohse, Frederick W. (2014). *Matayoshi Kobudo: A Brief History and Overview*. https://kodokanboston.files.wordpress.com/2014/02/meibukanmagazine-no-9_matayoshi.pdf

[9] Masahiro Nakamoto (1983). *Okinawa dentō kobudō : sono rekishi to tamashii*. Naha-shi, Bunbukan.

[10] Motokatsu Inoue (1972). Ryukyu Kobujutsu (Jou kan, Chu kan, & Ge kan) (Japanese only)

[11] Motokatsu Inoue (1989). Ryukyu Kobujutsu (Ten no maki & Chi no maki) (English and Japanese)

[12] Nail, Jim. "The Forbidden Art." *Black Belt Magazine*, Nov. 1982, pp. 76-80.

[13] Nishiuchi's Traditional Okinawan Kobudo Weaponry Series: Vol 11 - Mastering the Suruchin (Whip Rope). Century. (DVD)

[14] Patrick McCarthy (1999). *Ancient Okinawan Martial Arts: Koryu Uchinadi, Vol. 1*. Tuttle Martial Arts. ISBN-13 : 978-0804820936.

[15] Russo, Christian (2019). *Hojojutsu: The Warrior's Art of the Rope*. Yoshin Ryu Editions, Turin (Italy). ISBN-13: 978-8894232820

[16] Seiko, Fujita (1964). *Zuki Torinawajutsu*. http://www.freepdf.info/index.php?post/Fujita-Seiko-Zukai-Torinawajutsu

[17] Seiko, Fujita & Shahan, Eric Michael (2020), *Samurai Bondage*.. ISBN-13: 978-1950959112

[18] Shinken, Taira (2009 translated). *Encyclopedia of Okinawan Weapons*. ISBN-10 : 0920129242

[19] Shinpo, Matayoshi (2008). *Matayoshi Shinpo's Traditional Okinawan Kobudo*. Rising Sun Productions. DVD.

[20] Wubei Zhi (section with meteor hammer; page 560 of PDF). http://www.freepdf.info/index.php?post/Yuanyi-Mao-Wubei-Zhi-31-40

[21] https://ryukyukobudoshinkokai.wordpress.com/ryukyu-kobudo-weapons/ (...*The Ryukyu Kobudo Shinkokai inherited the long suruchin kata developed by Taira Shinken sensei (Maezato no suruchin) and the short suruchin kata developed by Minowa Katsuhiko sensei (Minowa no suruchin)*.) Retrieved 3-13-2021.

[22] Dr. Yang, Jwing-Ming (1999). *Ancient Chinese Weapons: A Martial Artist's Guide*. ISBN-13: 9781886969674

Index of Figures

Figure 1 Xie Zhen, the Two-headed Snake (Ryotoda Kaichin), from the series One Hundred and Eight Heroes of the Popular Shuihuzhuan (Tsuzoku Suikoden goketsu hyakuhachinin no hitori) 1827-30, Boston Museum of Fine Arts 2

Figure 2 1800's Illustration from Water Margin; story written late 14th century. http://gmzm.org/gudaizihua/shuihurenwu/index.asp?page=15 10

Figure 3 Tiara Shinken 11

Figure 4 Boys with Suruchin, from nanto zatsuwa (1880) 14

Figure 5 Ufuchiku, who reportedly practiced suruchin [12] 15

Figure 6 Taira Shinken, Motokatsu Inoue, Higa Seiko, and Matayoshi Shinpo (1960) 16

Figure 7 Fishing net and weights detail from Karwar, courtesy of Salil Nadkarni 16

Figure 8 Ryukyu Kobudo lineage 18

Figure 9 Taira Shinken 20

Figure 10 Eisuke Akamine 20

Figure 11 Motokatsu Inoue 20

Figure 12 Akamine Hiroshi 20

Figure 13 Yukio Kuniyoshi 21

Figure 14 Kisho Inoue 21

Figure 15 Moden Yabiku 21

Figure 16 Minowa Katsuhiko 21

Figure 17 Kenichi Yamashiro 24

Figure 18 Andrea Guarelli 24

Figure 19 Matayoshi Kobudo lineage 24

Figure 20 Shinko Matayoshi 25

Figure 21 Shinpo Matayoshi 25

Figure 22 Shinjo Gima Portrait 25

Figure 23 Yasushi Matayoshi 25
Figure 24 Meteor Hammer - By Samuraiantiqueworld - Own work, CC BY-SA 3.0, https://commons.wikimedia.org/w/index.php?curid=12682113 26
Figure 25 Wubei Zhi 1621 - meteor hammers 27
Figure 26 Example of various Chinese meteor hammer end weights, later Qing era. Courtesy of the Neil Anderson Collection, of antiquechinesesword.com. 28
Figure 27 Later Qing era garlic head mace, brass 14.1oz. Courtesy of the Neil Anderson Collection, of antiquechinesesword.com 28
Figure 28 Engraving describing Shaolin 8-9ft meteor hammer of Qing dynasty. 29
Figure 29 Meteor hammer painting. Courtesy of the Neil Anderson Collection, of antiquechinesesword.com 29
Figure 30 Xie Zhen, the Two-headed Snake (Ryotoda Kaichin), from the series One Hundred and Eight Heroes of the Popular Shuihuzhuan (Tsuzoku Suikoden goketsu hyakuhachinin no hitori) 1827-30, Boston Museum of Fine Arts 30
Figure 31 Emeric Essex Vidal (1791-1861), Public domain, via Wikimedia Commons 31
Figure 32 Illustration from the Water Margin story, Shui hu ren wu quan tu by Du Jin, 1467-1487 32
Figure 33 Illustration from History of the Three Kingdoms, 1368-1644, World Digital Library 33
Figure 34 Rante of Indonesia [4], Copyright © 1972 by Charles E Tuttle Publishing Co., Inc. 34
Figure 35 Suruchin length 37
Figure 36 Rope and Stone Suruchin, author's collection 38
Figure 37 Metal weights, courtesy of Todd Ward 39
Figure 38 Additional example of rope suruchin 39
Figure 39 Rope suruchin with Matayoshi style handle, courtesy of Todd Ward 39

Figure 40 Dr.mgf.winkelmann, Copyrighted free use, via Wikimedia Commons 40

Figure 41 Hag stone, authors collection - from USA East coast 41

Figure 42 Traditional chain suruchins of karatekobudopalau.com 43

Figure 43 Suruchin with barbs, courtesy of http://bushukan.wp.xdomain.jp/ 43

Figure 44 suruchin from jin-1.juttemaster.gozaru.jp 44

Figure 45 Taira lineage suruchins, of ryukyukobujutsuhozonshinkokai.org 44

Figure 46 Chain Suruchin Photo: paazio / flickr 45

Figure 47 Suruchin made from Manriki 46

Figure 48 Barbed suruchin, with details of construction 47

Figure 49   Top Left: Meteor hammer style handle.   Top Right: Barbed end. Bottom: Chain suruchin. Courtesy of Todd Ward 48

Figure 50 Modern monkey fist suruchin 49

Figure 51 Youth Hemp suruchin 49

Figure 52 Iron ball and Dyneema® Suruchin 50

Figure 53 Kashaka style suruchin 53

Figure 54 Traditional Kashaka; photozou: Ludwig D. Omen, CC BY 2.1 JP, via Wikimedia Commons 53

Figure 55 3/4" ball bearing suruchin 54

Figure 56 Tennis ball suruchin 55

Figure 57 Cotton rope/wooden bead suruchin 55

Figure 58 Handle-type practice short suruchin 56

Figure 59 Fishing weight suruchin 56

Figure 60 Pocket Suruchin (collapsed) 57

Figure 61 Pocket suruchin (expanded) 57

Figure 62 Pocket suruchin parts list 59

Figure 63 Construction of pocket suruchin 61

Figure 64 Wrapping for storage 61

Figure 65 Captive prisoner before magistrate, 1870 by Shimooka Renjō 62

Figure 66 Japanese prisoner, late 1800's 62

Figure 67 Seiko Fujita, Zukai Torinawajutsu author 1898 – 1966 63
Figure 68 Capturing technique, from Zukai Torinawajutsu 63
Figure 69 Rope coil, from Zukai Torinawajutsu 64
Figure 70 Kamagakushi, from Zukai Torinawajutsu 66
Figure 71 Hayanawa technique 1, from Zukai Torinawajutsu [16] 69
Figure 72 Hayanawa technique 2, from Zukai Torinawajutsu [16] 70
Figure 73 Taira Shinken with suruchin 119
Figure 74 Motokatsu Inoue demonstrating bunkai, courtesy of Victor Smith. 141
Figure 75 Matayoshi Shinpo demonstrating suruchin technique, courtesy of www.bushikan.com 161
Figure 76 Kobudo Dummy 231
Figure 77 Spot markers 232
Figure 78 PVC Target 232
Figure 79 Begleri, used with permission from www.aroundsquare.com 233

Made in United States
Cleveland, OH
07 January 2025